ILLUSTRATIONS

OF

GESTURE AND ACTION.

PRACTICAL

ILLUSTRATIONS

OF

RHETORICAL GESTURE

AND ACTION.

by

Henry Siddons

Second Edition,
first published London, 1822
Reissued 1968 by
Benjamin Blom, Inc.
New York

PRACTICAL ILLUSTRATIONS

OF

Rhetorical Gesture and Action;

ADAPTED TO

THE ENGLISH DRAMA:

FROM A WORK ON THE SUBJECT BY M. ENGEL,

MEMBER OF THE ROYAL ACADEMY OF BERLIN.

BY HENRY SIDDONS.

Embellished with Sixty-nine Engravings,

EXPRESSIVE OF THE VARIOUS PASSIONS, AND REPRESENTING THE MODERN
COSTUME OF THE LONDON THEATRES.

Second Edition, Improved.

LONDON:

PRINTED FOR SHERWOOD, NEELY, AND JONES,

PATERNOSTER ROW.

1822.

First published in a second,
improved edition London 1822
Reissued 1968,
by Benjamin Blom, Inc. Bx 10452

Library of Congress Catalog Card No. 67-18425

PREFACE

TO THE SECOND EDITION.

————

THE much approved work of Mr. HENRY
SIDDONS, as it is expressed in the title
page, originated with the learned and ingenious M. ENGEL, whose Treatise on Gesture and Theatrical Action in the German
language had long been known and de-
servedly esteemed on the Continent. It
may be said, with justice, to contain most
luminous views relative to the human passions, and to reduce to scientific principles
the ART OF PUBLIC SPEAKING.

Such a work was obviously a desideratum
in the English language ; and a translation
of M. Engel's Treatise might have been
sufficient to supply it, if his principles in
the original work had not been peculiarly
adapted to the business of the German
stage, and his references and examples
chiefly taken from the drama of that country.

Thus situated, it became an essential duty in the Editor to anglicise the matter, as well as translate the language of his author :—but in performing this task, the general sentiments and opinions of M. Engel were scrupulously retained; though, in every particular application of them, great care was taken to give the work, in its new form, all the interest of which it was susceptible to the English reader.

The present Edition has also been enriched with the observations contained in Mr. Sharpe's ESSAY ON GESTURE, in which the improvements (entirely English) will be found numerous and characteristic. This was lately delivered before a Philosophical Society, and received with great applause.

In the present Edition, the plates have been more conveniently arranged, and increased in number; and the Costume of the London Theatres has been illustrated by appropriate passages from some of our most popular dramas.

London, Nov. 1821.

Pride

Contempt.

Contempt

Suspicion

SUSPICION

Phlegm

Phlegm

Hauteur

Hauteur

Idiotism.

Idiotism

Sinking to repose

Sinking to repose

Starting from repose.

Starting from repose

Doubt

Doubt

Apprehension

Apprehension

Painful recollection

Painful Recollection

Scorn

Scorn

Sublime admiration

Sublime Admiration

Astonishment

Astonishment

Devotion.

Devotion

Affection.

Affection

Terror

Terror

Voluptuary

A voluptuary

Thirst

Thirst

Expectation

Expectation

Terror

from Lairesse

Terror, from Lairesse

Terror
(as described by Engel.)

Terror, as described by Engel

Horror

Horror

Voluptuous Indolence

Voluptuous Indolence

Joy.

Joy

Conceit

Conceit

Vulgar Arrogance

Vulgar Arrogance

False Gesture

False Gesture

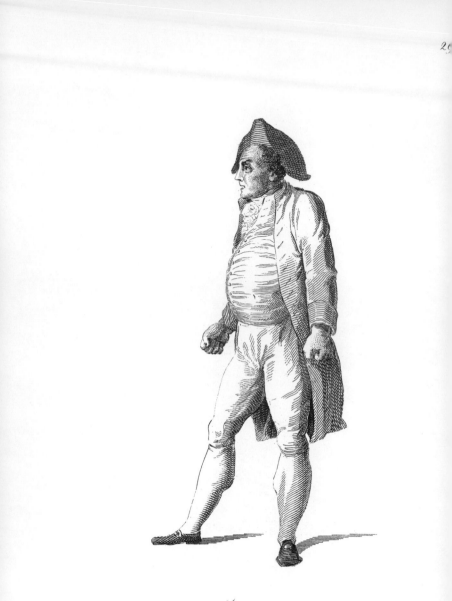

Menace

Menace

Dejection

Dejection

False Gesture

False Gesture

False Gesture

False Gesture

False Gesture

False Gesture.

Love

Love

Jealous Rage

Jealous Rage

Servility

Servility

Loftiness

Loftiness

39

Tranquil Joy

Tranquil Joy

Quietude

Quietude

Anger

Anger

Despondency

Despondency

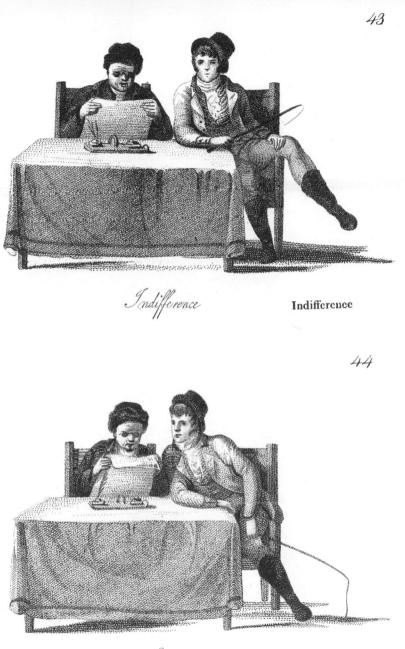

Indifference

Indifference

Expectation

Expectation

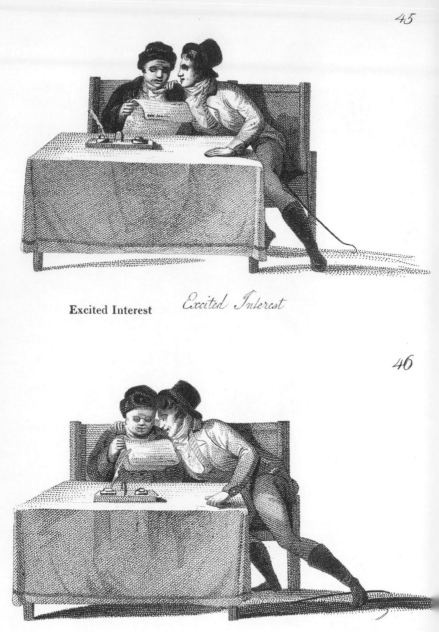

Excited Interest *Excited Interest*

Gratification

Gratification

Despair

Despair

Enthusiasm

Enthusiasm

Distraction & Persuasion

Distraction and Persuasion.

Persuasion repulsed

Persuasion repulsed

Reproach

Reproach

Supplication

Supplication

Fallen greatness

Fallen Greatness.

Sickness

Sickness

Conciet

Conceit

Vulgar triumph

What will Mrs Grundy say?

Vulgar Triumph

Hopeless Love

Hopeless Love

Vulgar Astonishment

Vulgar Astonishment

Obsequiousness

Obsequiousness

Rustic Cunning

Rustic Cunning

Bajazet

Bajazet

Foppery

Foppery

Mirth

Mirth

Agility

Agility

Sublime Adoration

Rolla.

Adoration

Hearty Welcome

Hearty Welcome

Fashionable Impudence

Fashionable Impudence

A Discovery

A Discovery

Obsequious attention

Obsequious Attention

ILLUSTRATIONS

OF

GESTURE AND ACTION.

LETTER I.

On the Possibility of the practical Illustration of Gesture and Action.

THE arguments, by which you have endeavoured to persuade me to give up my ideas of a Treatise on the Defects and Proprieties of the Dress and Action now adopted in our Theatres, have produced an effect on my mind entirely opposite to the sentiments you wished to excite. So far from convincing me of my error, they have tended to *root* my original opinion more deeply. This, you will say, is the way in which every self-willed blockhead conducts himself; the more one shows him the folly or impracticability of his projects, with the greater obstinacy is he sure to pursue them. Although I flatter myself, my dear friend, that I do not exactly deserve this reproach from you, yet I cannot resist a strong impulse which I feel, to pursue the subject a little farther, if it be only to convince myself, that there really is nothing so very *absurd* or *extravagant* in the ideas which I formerly communicated to you.

Our theatres have lately made such rapid strides towards perfection in the article of *costume*, that we may reasonably expect the completion of our hopes. If ever a liberal and discerning public had a right to look for this perfection in their favourite amusement, it is at the present moment. When the august monarch of this nation honours every one with his countenance who makes an effort for the improvement of the drama, it would be shameful, indeed, if those who are versed in the science did not exert every faculty, to co-operate in removing all obstructions in the way of its progression and improvement. You tell me, that every thing which is executed by *prescribed rules* will be *formal, stiff, embarrassed,* and *precise.* You will please to observe how I endeavour to answer this objection. While the rule is perpetually present to the mind of the scholar, he will, perhaps, be awkward and confused in all his gestures, and the fear of making constant mistakes will render him more constrained and irresolute than if he were to give way to his habitual actions. I will grant you thus much with great willingness, but you will in return allow *me* one grand and general position, viz. that use is a second nature. A man when he first learns to *dance*, moves with a solemnity which approaches the ridiculous; but this solemnity in time wears off, and his step becomes not only more majestic, but more sure, more free, and more unembarrassed than his who has never practised that accomplishment. Should you state, in reply to this, that the same argument will hold good in the mere *exercise* of the profession of an actor, I answer, that though the general rule be allowed, that habit becomes a kind of nature; yet the same rule will have equal place with regard to *awkward* as well as *elegant* actions. A constant custom of appearing before the public may make a man bold, but between *grace* and *boldness* there is as wide a difference as there is between *light* and *darkness*.

Do not think me, however, so absolutely devoted to my own theory as to be totally insensible to the objections you have made to the practicable part of my system. Some of your arguments are weighty, and I own they have put me to some trouble in my efforts to remove them. No science was ever yet brought to any perfection without much labour in surmounting difficulties, and I only demand a requisite degree of patience in the examination of mine. Your chief objection to my plan is sensible, and, I must confess, is founded on the principles of nature and of reason. If I understand your argument aright, you mean to say, that the same expression or modification of a passion is delineated by various ways in various persons, without a necessity of any *one* of those modes being superior to the *other;* and that we must likewise consider the personages in their characters, national and private, the age and sex, and the thousand complex *&cs.* belonging to them, before we can safely say what is the *best* expression or modification of a peculiar passion.

Your objection, thus interpreted and explained, I own, carries a great weight with it, and merits a very serious consideration on my part.

LETTER II.

On the Variety of Manners in different Parts of the World—
The European—The Inhabitants of Oriental Countries—
The Origin of the Cap of Liberty—Different Degrees of
Expressions of Amity and Affection.—The Courtier and
the Cottager.—The Study of History recommended.

You ask me wherefore I lay so much stress upon
the *one* particular objection of yours with which
I concluded my last letter? You also demand
why I single *it* from the numberless others, as
meriting a serious disquisition? It is because
that peculiar objection seems to indicate the true
mode by which the theory of *theatrical* action is
to be more fully developed.

It is very true that the inhabitants of various
countries have different modes of expressing the
same passions, and that this difference is often
strikingly obvious.

The European, when he would give a mark
of respect, takes off his hat; the inhabitant of
the East keeps *his head covered*, under the same
circumstances. The former expresses the very
highest degree of veneration and humility towards an acknowledged superior, by a bend of

the head, and a trivial inclination of the back—
he rarely bows the knee. The other, in the same
predicament, muffles up his visage, and falls pros-
trate on the earth. The uncovering of the head
amongst the Europeans is by no means a natural expression, but simply a mere allusion to some
ancient and arbitrary custom. Probably it al-
ludes to that of the Romans, who never allowed
their slaves to carry any covering for the head
till they had been legally affranchised; and, for
this reason, the bonnet or cap is unto this day
the symbol of liberty.

To veil and cover up the face is a natural expression, and carries the idea of respect and veneration to its very climax. It is equally the sign
of shame and modesty. In short, it is the most
humble mode of avowing the sense of our own
unworthiness, when weighed against the superior
and more lofty qualifications of another. Shame
and modesty have the same affinity to each other
which subsists between fear and veneration: for
this reason, the European, naturally cold, expresses this latter sentiment either by modestly
inclining his eyes towards the ground, or by
seldom raising them without an appearance of
timidity. Let the mind, however, abstract itself
from these characteristical shades; let it endea-

vour to do away the allusion to an ancient custom in the European, and the more exalted
enthusiasm of the inhabitant of the Oriental
countries, and the truly *natural* and *essential* part
of the sentiment will yet remain; to wit, the
motion of the body. This expression is carried
to its highest pitch, when a man extends himself
on the ground, with his face in contact with the
earth. The most slight mark of the *same* expression is when he confines himself to a simple
motion of the head. I conclude, therefore, that
this sign is *natural* and *essential*, because it is
general, and holds place with all people, with all
nations, without distinction of their ranks, their
estates, or their conditions; though I grant that
it admits of a wide and infinite variety of shades
and circumflexions. I do not know any one
country on the face of the earth, any one class of
men who would strive to express esteem, respect,
or veneration, by lifting up their heads, or seem-
ing to give an additional height to their stature;
as, on the contrary, I am inclined to believe that
there is no nation or body of men who do not
express pride and contempt by a deportment exactly the reverse; that is to say, by an exaltation
of the head, by a straightening of the back, and
sometimes erecting themselves on their toes, to

give an air more commanding and imposing to the general contour of the figure.

If the general character of countries causes a variety in the expression of the passions, this expression is equally modified by the character proper for each sex, and for each age, as well as by the individual qualities of each man in particular. The characteristical determinations of the moral nature and the organization of the body may *vary* the manners, sentiments, and expressions in a thousand ways, without occasioning any alteration in the grand *essence*. One is impetuous, another is indolent; while the first expresses his irritability, the other remains *immovable*. Impatience makes the former throw his body into a thousand contortions, while the same sentiment in the latter only displays itself in his physiognomy. That which makes the one man laugh aloud till his sides ache with the exertion, only raises a smile, hardly visible, on the lip of his opposite.

The same observation holds good with regard to the variety of states. The squeeze of the hand, the kiss, and the embrace, are three different modes of expressing amity and affection.— The first is the *weakest*, because it simply joins two extremities of the human body to each other.

The last is the most forcible, because it in a manner draws together and incorporates the object with oneself. The great, with whom *politeness* is now become a species of *virtue*, have digested a code of laws of their own, wherein they introduce all these signs of amity into what they are pleased to denominate civility and good breeding. They generally outstep the modesty of nature in these expressions, adapting the strongest of them to the most trifling occasions. They talk of *transport*, when the simple word *pleasure* would signify more than they really *feel;* they bow to the very ground, when a slight inclination of the head would be adequate to the occasion. They dart into each other's arms with rapture, when advancing a few steps would express all the *real* pleasure they can be supposed to experience in their meeting.

The inhabitant of the country, that child, cherished by parent Nature, whose heart the manners of large cities has not yet vitiated nor abased, knows also the value of an *embrace;* but he reserves this last token of affection for the period of undissembled transport; till the happy moment when a long-absent son returns to his paternal roof. He expresses the common intercourses of friendship by a simple pressure of the *hand;* but when the *heart* is really concerned, he is all fire, all energy, all force !

You see that we have here a general and essential trait—a *tendency to approach* and to *unite* to each other—the natural consequences of intimacy and friendship ; all the differences of which, in various classes of society, are solely indicated by the different degrees of intimacy and union, as also by some secondary modifications depending on the polished modes of rough manners, on the warmth and heat of constitution, and a thousand other accidental variations in the passions, sentiments, opinions, and organization of individuals. It is upon these general, natural, and essential traits, that (in my opinion) it would be possible to form a system of the highest possible utility to those engaged in a theatrical pursuit.

The player who wishes to be accomplished in his art should not only study the passions on their broad and general basis ; he should trace their operations in all their shades, in all their different varieties, as they act upon different conditions, and as they operate in various climates. The perusal of history, and an attention to the several collections of voyages and travels which have been made, will enable an intelligent player to form some idea of countries far distant, of ages long past. This is a most necessary study for a comedian; this alone can give him an idea of the exact manners and customs of different nations, and at different times. The more he reasons over his task, the wider will his knowledge extend: he will find his imagination expanded by these studies. The consciousness of a proper knowledge of his subject will give confidence to his demeanour, persuasion to his accents, and a general eloquence to all he says or does.

LETTER III.

Perfection more requisite to the Actor than to other Artists—His Advantages and Difficulties—An Imitation of Nature recommended—Servile Copying to be shunned—Beauty of a great Actress, in delineating the Agonies of Death—Farther Remarks on this Head—Hints to the Ladies concerning an Overviolence in the Representation of particular Passions—General Reflections.

It appears to me, my dear friend, that the tables are completely turned.   How is this? You! you who, a short time ago, laughed at my theory, as absurd and impracticable, *now* give me the greatest encouragement to proceed in my plan!   All the comedians, you say, will be greatly obliged to me:—of that I know nothing.   I agree with you, however, that there is no artist to whom perfection ought to appear more important than to the *actor ;* because none enjoys the favour of the public in a manner more prompt, more pleasing, or more brilliant.   You will likewise say, that there is no artist who is a witness of the criticisms made on his talent in a way so public and so humiliating ; not only because the disgrace is testified as openly as the triumph, but add to this, that the victim is forced to be present at his own immolation, and cannot, like the celebrated painter of antiquity, hide himself behind a curtain, to hear what the judges say of his works. This circumstance may serve to explain why a public performer is more alive to the darts of criticism than other artists. But how can we account for that apathy, that incurious negligence, which is so prevalent among the generality of them. How comes it that they do not aim more strongly at perfection? that they strive not to form themselves in all the different branches of their art, by reading, by reflection, and by a better chosen society? The greater part of them are enchanted by the ignorance and bad taste of the public. They would rather (to use a forcible phrase) *usurp* the applause of an audience, foment theatrical cabals, and, governed by a base jealousy, seize on every principal character, whether adapted to their peculiar abilities or not, to keep their rivals out of sight, than strive to deserve the approbation of the judicious, by the real merit of their acting. I much fear that lessons, delivered in a public manner, will be more calculated to excite their *anger* than their *gratitude;* for in the act of giving information to them, the public is enlightened at the same time. In the great number of these artists, it is but justice to own, that there are some who think and act in a more noble manner. To *these*, then, I shall address the following pages.

To render my work less difficult, I ought to begin it by *classing* the different modifications of the human form, which the actor studies after nature. They consist of two principal species : in those which are solely founded on the mechanism of the *body ;* as, for example, a difficulty of respiration after running rapidly, and the sinking of the eyelids at the approach of sleep, &c. &c. &c. and in those which, more depending on the co-operation of the *soul,* serve as mediums to judge of its affections, its movements, and its desires, as occasional *motives* and *causes.* It would be ridiculous to make a scrupulous and faithful enumeration of the former ; for every one knows that sleep closes the eyelids.

There are but two counsels to give the actor on this head : first, that he ought to seize all occasions of observing nature, even in those effects which are unfrequent in their occurrence ; and, in the second place, that he should never lose sight of the main end and grand design of his art, by shocking the spectator with too coarse or too servile an imitation.

If the first actress now on our stage had never

been present at the bed of a dying person, her acting, under such circumstances, might probably have lost one of its most natural and affecting traits.

It is remarked, says a celebrated foreign author, that persons in the agonies of death have a custom of *pinching*, and gently drawing to and fro their garments.

Our actress has made the most happy use of this remark.   At the moment when her soul is supposed to be just ready to quit her body, she gives signs of a slight convulsion, but this is apparent only at the ends of her fingers : she nips up her robe; and the arm, in that action, suddenly seems numbed and powerless ; the last effort of a smouldering flame, the expiring beam of a sun just ready to set.

With regard to the second piece of advice, I would give one rule, which, I believe, has been frequently adduced before ; –that the agonies and approaches of death ought not to be represented with all the horrors which attend these dreadful moments in nature. The judicious player will soften down these horrors.   His head should have more the appearance of a man sinking to a sound sleep than of a person convulsed with strong agonies ; the voice should be broken and

altered, but not so as to give the effect of a disgusting rattling : in a word, an actor ought to
acquire a manner of his own, in representing the
last sigh of expiring mortality.   He should give
such an idea of death as every man would wish to
feel at that crisis ; though, perhaps, no one ever
will have the good fortune to find that wish accomplished.   Contemplate (if you can find patience for the task) the abominable grimaces and
unnatural distortions in which some players indulge themselves under similar circumstances,
and you will acknowledge the justice of this rule.
I have myself seen a *Macbeth* die in convulsions,
which were certainly very naturally imitated, but
at the same time have thrown the spectators into
convulsions of laughter, equally natural with his
own.   I would advise such a comedian to read
and reconsider the many excellent rules delivered
by the Roman satirist ; and, amongst the rest, to
observe the following :

> Nec pueros coram populo Medea trucidet
> Aut humana palam coquat exta-*nefarius Atreus.*
>
> Quæcunq; ostendis mihi sic-*incredulus odi.*

I do not know what evil genius persuades so
many of our performers, the females in particular,
that it is so exquisite a manœuvre to be perpetu-

ally rolling themselves on the ground. A lady acting Juliet, or any other character of that description, will sometimes fall on the boards with such violence, when she hears of the death or banishment of her lover, that we are really alarmed, lest her poor skull should be fractured by the violence of the concussion. Applause gained by arts so unnatural and so disgusting can only come from the ignorant and injudicious, who, incapable of forming a judgment on the real merit or interest of a touching situation, would be just as much concerned in the fate of a Punchinello or a Harlequin. If, on such an occurrence, an *amateur* be sometimes induced to join *his* suffrage to the general plaudit of the house, it is by a natural transition from contempt to pity: he is enchanted to find that the poor creature (who, though a most execrable actress, may be a very good girl for all that) has drawn herself out of her dangerous predicament, with all her limbs safe and sound. These feats of agility, these perilous leaps and jumps, are beneath the dignity even of a *legitimate* pantomime, which represents an *action*, and whose object is to excite both *interest* and attention: they are only proper to posture-masters at a fair, where, all the interest being centred in the *individual* alone, and on his *cor-*

poreal pliability, this interest rises the higher, the more imminent the danger to which he exposes himself. The modifications of the body, which depend upon the cooperation of the soul, and which manifest themselves in a manner more or less imposing, often have a signification extremely vague and general : they answer to the inflexions of the voice, which should be managed with so much nicety as to fix the attention of the auditor to the *same point* which employs that of the speaker. But this method of exciting the attention must be aided by another, more marking, more rapid, and more determinable—that is to say, by a method which may strike with greater force upon the *senses ;* as, for example, by the raising or sinking of the voice—by a pronunciation more slow and more imposing—or by a particular tone, marked and emphatical, on the *word* indicating the *idea* peculiarly worthy of this distinction.

However feeble this mode may appear at the first blush, its utility has been confirmed by long practice and experience ; the mind which feels its own resources will never fail to have recourse to it, more especially if that mind be aided and assisted by a well tuned voice. If the inflexion or tone of the voice comes sometimes to aid at-

tention, *action* or *gesture* will certainly have the
same effect; as, for example, the hand spread out,
the arm extended to its full length, the " Manus minus arguta, digitis subsequens verba, non
exprimens (the) brachium procerius projectum,
quasi quoddam telum oratoris."—*Cicero de Orat.*
l. iii. c. 59.

The gently striking of one hand against the
other; a slight movement of the head, which indicates a wish to dwell on such or such a word :
all these means may be employed to aid the elu-
cidation of a particular idea. The rule by which
this kind of *action* should be governed is the same
to which the accents and tones of the voice ought
to be limited. For as the actor ought to employ
the aid of emphasis for *principal* words alone,
without accenting them *all* with the same precision, which would render them confused, pompous, and ridiculous, so in his actions he ought
to retain their force for such passages as more
immediately require them. A perpetual seesaw
of the arms, such as we observe in schoolboys
when repeating their set speeches, fatigues the
eye by its insipidity, as much as an indiscrimi-
nate emphasis on every word, in a long sentence,
fatigues and disgusts a well governed ear by its

tiresomeness and monotony. " Any thing so overdone is from the purpose of playing."—*Shakspeare.*

I fear I have rather fatigued than amused you by my observations, which may appear somewhat trivial in your eyes. But, not to overburden you all at once, I shall reserve the general reflections which are to be made on the gestures and movements of the human body for another epistle.

LETTER IV.

On Gesture picturesque—and Gesture expressive—Of the Muscles and the Eyes—The Mouth—Of Redness and Paleness—Of Crying and Laughing—The Botanist and Physiognomist—Their Modes of Study similar to each other.

ALL modifications of the body, at all particular or determined, are to be divided into two ranks or classes—the gestures *picturesque*, and the gestures *expressive*. The seat of these gestures is not fixed to this or that particular portion of the body ; the soul exercises an equal power over all the muscles, as you have observed that every one of them may be figuratively said to speak in the celebrated statue of Laocoon. But this expression is, in some sort, too weak in certain particular muscles, compared with various others easy to be remarked. Besides, there are some parts too much covered by the drapery for every light and rapid expression to be discovered. The countenance is the principal seat of the movements of the soul—the most eloquent parts of the visage are the eyes, the eyebrows, the forehead, the mouth, the nose; in short, the *whole head,* as well as the neck, the shoulders, the hands, and the feet : there is no change of posture which may not have its particular expression or indication. The sentiments of Le Brun contradict the general opinion of the *eye* being the most eloquent part of the countenance. According to this painter, the *eyebrow* is the most faithful interpreter of the passions. For my own part, I am more inclined to side with Pliny, who gives a decided preference to the eye. You will please to remark, that there is a general rule which determines the expression, and by which (to a certain degree) we may generally measure the extent or vivacity of a sentiment. The soul speaks the most frequently, and most easily, in those parts where the muscles are *pliable* and *ductile;* of course she is most eloquent through the medium of those which compose the countenance—she speaks, consequently, most frequently in the *eyes.* These operate so spontaneously, and so easily, that they hardly leave an interval between the sentiment and its effect. The most reflective mind, the most determined sang froid, cannot arrest the momentary explosion, though they can, in some degree, regulate and control every other movement of the body.

The man who wishes to conceal the predominant passions of his soul ought to guard, above all things, against allowing them to fix in his *eyes*. Let him be equally careful of some of the muscles approaching the mouth, which are very difficult to master and command. Notwithstanding the soul always preserves some power over the muscles, she has none over the *blood*, says *Descartes;* and this is the reason why sudden redness and paleness are always independent of our will. If, then, the face and, above all, the eyes have this incontestible advantage in the expression of all which passes in the interior of the soul, what a pity that it should be so difficult to describe and note their changes and effects!

The French philosopher I have just quoted points out the reason of this extreme difficulty : " There exists no passion," says he, " which may not be denoted by some particular movement of the eye. This movement is sometimes so strikingly marked that the most stupid lackey can read in it the satisfaction or the anger of his master. But though these movements of the visionary nerves may be easily remarked, and their significations may be tolerably clear, it is still no easy labour to define them with *exactitude* and *precision.* Each of them depend on infinite varieties and numberless mutations, which are so curiously and finely blended that to distinguish and separate them is a labour frequently approximating to an impossibility."

One might nearly say the same thing of all the other expressive marks of the face; for though some have less of fineness than the eyes, yet it still requires a great portion of labour and difficulty to analyze and define them. They so frequently vary, and confound themselves one with the other, that there are some men who, in crying, make use of the same muscles which are employed by others whilst they are laughing.

But you will doubtless say, What is the use of this scrupulous mode of examining every different *ramification* of a gesture? It would be much better to have clear and distinct denominations —such as would lie within the scope of every capacity. I grant it would be a great advantage, if we did possess these defined terms. But all languages are at present so meagre that to give even *simple ideas* on the subject in question is by no means an easy undertaking. Yet let us not entirely give up a hope founded on reason and possibility—a hope that some accomplished artist may, one day or other, supply the defects of language, and give us intelligible rules for the practice of this difficult theorem. While reflecting, says Sulzer, that, by the sole examination of drawings and descriptions, an amateur in natural history is able to imprint the shape of many thousand plants and insects in his mind, with such exactitude and precision that he can mark the slightest variations in their structures—the most minute deviation in their anatomical parts —we may with reason conclude, that a collection of different physiognomies, collected and classed with the same industry, is a scheme equally possible, and that a new art would result from the attempt, not less important in its kind. Why would not a collection of expressive gestures and attitudes be as easy as a collection of drawings, plants, or shells? And if this affair should one day become an object of serious study, why should not technical words be in time found out, as proper for *this* science as those at present discovered for the facilitation of the study of natural history?

I am sure you will not be the man to com-

pare the science of selecting butterflies and
shells with an art which, if it should ever rise to
any eminence, will be employed in the investiga-
tion of the noblest portion of Heaven's noblest
work—the erect, the contemplative, the sublime
countenance of its own image—*man!*

LETTER V.

Of the Beautiful—And the Natural or True—The two Ques-
tions reunited—Nature beyond Art in a Player—The
Rules of Riccoboni.

IF the gestures are the exterior and visible signs
of our bodies, by which the interior modifications
of the soul are manifested and made known, it
follows that we may consider them under a double point of view : In the first place, as visible
changes of themselves ;—secondly, as the means
indicative of the interior operations of the soul.
This double point of view gives occasion for a
double question. *Art* will demand an answer to
this interrogation—In the first place—What is
beautiful ?—In the second place it will inquire,
What is *natural,* or *true ?*   Now, neither the
one nor the other of these questions is to be neglected.   Art will reunite them into a single proposition, and will ask—What is at the same time
the *most beautiful* and the *most true ?*

Go over all the particular rules which have
been laid down concerning the action of the
orator, and even of the comedian, and you will

find, to the great disadvantage of the art, that
the practitioners have cultivated the *first* requisite much more than the *second.* Thus the
greater part of the traditional rules concerning
theatrical declamation have no other object than
dignity or beauty.

From hence we derive that frigid eloquence
in the acting of so many of our performers, and
the minikin, dull, formal precision of several
others. Art is a great assistant, but nature is
the very *soul* of a player. Now nature differs
much in different men ; but what is natural in
one personage shall be ridiculous in another.
We have an actor on our own stage, who formerly played the comic and the tragic casts
alternately. This actor disdained the pompous
strut of his predecessors : when he attempted to
imitate the manners of gentlemen in private life,
he never endeavoured to tread with the mincing
axactitude of a dancing master, or to lay stress
on syllables, till he gave to trifles the dubious importance of oracles. Truth ought to be the guide
of every artist, and this principle has been the
general conductor of the excellent comic actor
to whom I allude. Beauty was likewise his
guide, but subordinate to his first grand principle. Without ever losing sight of truth or

nature, he blended them most happily together. When acting in tragedy he was not equally happy. Formed for the laughter-loving Muse, it was somewhat whimsical to see him assume the *Hero*, and, with his light utterance and airy form, go through characters of weight and consequence *.

But let us return to the bad effects which would fall on the comedian, if he were to follow the advice of those who are constantly importuning him to pay his *sole attention* to the grace of his attitudes. I shall quote a passage on this subject, which I think somewhat to the purpose.

Riccoboni has laid down some rules, in his Art of the Theatre, which would render that player a mere *pedant*, who should follow them to the *letter*. My object is not to make an enumeration of these rules here, or to refute them in the detail. I shall simply confine myself to the

---

* The truly excellent comedian here alluded to has long dropped the buskin of tragedy, and applies himself solely to a cast of character, wherein we read of no *predecessor* who has exceeded him, and know no *successor* to his well earned honours. Every true lover of the drama will join me in wishing that his course may be long as it has been brilliant, and that he may yet flourish many years, admired by the public, and respected by his friends.

motion of the hands, of which he speaks thus:
" In lifting up the arm, the superior part, *i. e.*
that from the shoulder to the elbow, ought to be
first elevated : the hand ought to be the last part
in action," &c. &c.

Is not all this a species of pedantry, and more
adapted to complete a set of puppets than to
form a race of great orators and accomplished
comedians ?

LETTER VI.

Gesture useful in the common Occurrences of Life—The Tutor and his Pupil—The Judge and the Accused—Horatian Maxim—On Objects of Grandeur and Sublimity—A Novice at a Play—Aristotle's Reason for the Superiority of a Man over a Monkey—Examples of imitative Gesture—The Rhetorical Footman—Synecdoche an Italian Gesture—Reflection on the Examination of Nature.

GESTURE may be of infinite utility in many of the occurrences of common life, an additional proof of its being indispensably necessary for carrying on the illusions of the *mimic world.* When a tutor wishes to convince his pupil of the indelicacy, the ridiculousness, or the awkwardness of any action, he practises them, with a little overcharging, before him. The boy sees his error as in a glass.—Volumes might be written on the subject, and never convince him so thoroughly as one spontaneous and well executed imitation of the fault committed. When a governess desires that her charge should acquire grace and dignity in her person and her movements, she makes her own air and deportment as exalted as possible, that she may illustrate her theory by the conviction of vision, and by the force of habit and imitation.

When an accused person tries to justify himself, before his judge, for having been led, in the heat of his passion, to strike the *first blow*, he endeavours, whilst reciting the cause of the quarrel, to *imitate* all the menaces, and all the offensive, irritating postures of his adversary (taking care to *exaggerate* them as much as possible) to convince the court that a man of honour had no other alternative but knocking down the person who thus outraged his feelings as a gentleman.

In these instances we find the causes of picturesque gestures reunited.

1. The representation of the fault committed by the scholar.

2. The beauty of a deportment, full of grace and dignity on the part of the governess.

3. The idea of the greatness of the provocation received by the accused person.

In these three cases, the *correction*, the *instruction*, and the *justification* require the aid of *picturesque gestures*, in all the persons concerned.

Neither of these ends could be attained but by an animated representation of its object, and the striking images of visible phenomena must, without doubt, be the most potent mode of expressing them in a sensible manner ; to this circumstance we may aptly apply the beautiful though well known observation of Horace :—

Segniùs irritant animos demissa per aurem,
Quàm quæ sunt oculis subjecta fidelibus, et quæ
Ipse sibi tradit Spectator.
De Arte Poet. ver. 180—182.

Experience proves that the force communicated by the representation of an object is capable of producing imitation in any *body*, where the mind is strongly occupied or attracted by it.

" An intuitive and complete representation of an action (says a very ingenious philosopher) is a predisposition to the action itself. While representing the idea of any words to ourselves, we pronounce them interiorly ; and, when this internal language becomes forcible, by acquiring a greater portion of vivacity, we begin to make motions with our lips."

This effect frequently continues augmenting

itself, until we really pronounce the words aloud, as if we wished to communicate them to some one, though we chance to be entirely alone.   In generalizing the proposition of this sage still farther, we may add, that each complete and intuitive representation of a thing (though the event or the thing be not a human action) is accompanied by an impulse, or an attraction, which leads us to the imitation of it.   Another philosopher has made this remark, with respect to the grand and the sublime.

" An object," says he, " which possesses grandeur, dilates the chest, and insensibly engages the spectator in an attempt to enlarge the proportions of his body.   This effect is particularly remarkable in those persons, who, despising social compacts, and the laws of politeness, abandon themselves entirely to the impulse of nature, while aiming at descriptions of grand objects. Governed at that moment by a natural instinct, they swell themselves out, and walk like persons inspired.   An object of *sublimity* produces another expression of sentiment.   It forces the spectator to an elevation of his body, even to the standing on tiptoe."

As there is nothing which can be more interesting to man than *himself*, and as he can represent nothing more perfectly than the modifications and qualities of the human body, of course they are naturally his chief and most favourite studies. When a person sits at the theatre, after having seen a play acted three or four times, his mind naturally becomes vacant and inactive. If among the spectators he chance to recognize a youth, to whom the same is new, this object affords him, and many others, a more entertaining fund of observation than all that is going forward on the stage.

This novice of an auditor, carried away by the illusion, imitates all he sees, even to the actions of the players, though in a mode less decisive. Without knowing what is going to be said, he is serious, or contented, according to the tone which the performers happen to take. His eyes become a mirror, faithfully reflecting the varying gestures of the several personages concerned.

Ill humour, irony, anger, curiosity, contempt, in a word, all the passions of the author are repeated in the lines of his countenance. This imitative picture is only interrupted whilst his proper sentiments, crossing exterior objects, seek for modes of expressing themselves. Such observations as these, which a man may make every day of his life, prove that Aristotle was perfectly right, when he ranked the man above the monkey, in affording him the superiority in the art of imitation. This observation on the *communicative* power of gesture is highly interesting to the actor in general, and to the *comedian* in particular; because he may draw great advantage from it, in rendering his *mute* play more animated.

I shall here endeavour to point out an observation, which is, in my opinion, of some moment. It concerns the great number of figures, particularly of metaphors, which abound in the dictionary of gestures, as well as in every other language, whether one aims at the picturesque or at the expressive. Every incomplete picture, above all of invisible objects, and of internal or intellectual ideas, ought to embody itself by *images*, which may be *thus* effected: On thinking of a soul replete with grandeur and sublimity, the body is elevated, the visage is exalted. If we have the idea of an *obstinate* character, we instantly assume a firm position, clench the fist, and stiffen the back. Imitation is effected by fine and delicate touches. I could produce a great quantity of examples for *Imitative Gesture.*

What think you of a *rhetorician* who substitutes the *effect* for the *cause?* The lackey, speaking of the unlucky reward his master may bestow on all his wild pranks, *rubs his back with the hind part of his hand,* as if he already felt the pain of the blows inflicted by him. Will you have another instance, which, instead of the *thing itself,* indicates an *exterior affinity?* To designate the true God, or the Gods of Paganism, the language of gesture intimates their residence in heaven, by pointing to the skies.

After the same manner, the hands elevated, the eyes directed to the celestial mansions, call the Gods to witness innocence, implore their assistance, and solicit their vengeance. Would you rather prefer a Synecdoche? One points out a single person present, meaning to represent a whole family: we show a sole enemy when we intend to give the idea of a hostile army.

Should you like to have an example of the IRONICAL? A young beauty, refusing the hand of a lover whom she despises, makes him a courtesy down to the ground. The number of *allusions*, with regard to gestures, will be found equally extensive.

The action of washing the hands gives the sign of innocence; two fingers on the forehead, the infidelity of a wife; blowing lightly over the palm of the hand, designates the idea of *nothing*. The *Italian*, who generally converses by gesture in a very animated manner, has (among others) a very expressive one; it is when he means to express his distrust of a man whom he suspects of being false and dissembling. *(See Plate* I.)

He then fixes his eye upon his object, with a side glance, highly expressive of his doubts; one hand is furtively thrust down by his side, with a full extension of his arm; the body is slightly turned towards the person whom he means to warn; the other hand, on the same side, draws down the cheek, that this eye may become more large than the other, which had already seemed less than it naturally was, by the expression of *distrust*. By this means he forms himself a *double profile*, and a countenance of which one part bears no manner of resemblance to its opposite. The one side, turned towards the suspected person, has all the appearance of diffidence; the pulling of the other cheek seems simply to serve the purpose of enlarging the eye, and the object of this magnitude seems to indicate the great attention necessary for him to use, in guarding against the tricks of a sharper.

The second figure represents another kind of pantomime, frequently resorted to by the Italian, when he wishes to express his contempt of a menace or a warning. He gently draws the back of his hand several times under his chin, and turns back his head with an ironical smile, as if deaf to the speaker, and concentrated in himself. It is singular that both these panto-mimes should be at the same time so very easy to *comprehend,* and yet so extremely difficult to *explain.*

Perhaps the Italian wishes to make known, by this gesture, that which the inhabitant of Germany means to insinuate by a particular phrase, the sense of which is, " nothing troubles me." Perhaps too he means to say that he thinks as little of the affair, the other has been making so serious and important, as he does of the dust which the wind happened to have blown on his beard. I candidly own my ignorance of the *precise* or *literal* explication, which is to be

given to the above mentioned pantomime, a confession I shall be frequently compelled to make,
even when very *simple* expressions are the theme,
expressions *common* with several distant nations.
The more we examine nature, the more matter
we find for observation; her secrets are incalcu-
lable: the *material* part of them escapes from
our view, and the *intellectual* portion surpasses
our penetration.

LETTER VII.

Analogous Gestures—Physiological Gestures—On the Deli-
neation of Passion—Shakspeare's Observation on the Sub-
ject—The Remark of Quintilian—The Weepers at ancient
Funerals—Advice to Tragedians.

You have reason on your side when you say that
a pantomime in Italy, written by a thinking genius, would make a very interesting work.

The theory of *this art*, like that of most others,
depends chiefly upon observation.

Your second idea, that our actors would gain
something by borrowing from those of Italy, appears equally well founded. They would find
in this nation a warmth, a fire, congenial to the
climate; a vivacity only to be found in those
countries where the blood circulates with vigour.

From *Picturesque Gestures*, on which head I
have little more of importance to add, I pass to
Expressive Gestures. These are so many, and
so complex, that I am almost tempted to class
them, in order to facilitate my disquisition.

Some of these gestures are *motive*, or made by *design*. Such are the exterior and voluntary motions by which we know the affections, the desires, the tendencies, and the passions of the souls, which they are the means of satisfying. To this class, for example, belong the *inclination* of the person towards the object which excites our interest. The attitude firm and prepared to attack an adversary, when angry—the arms extended in love—thrown back in fear, &c. &c. Other gestures are *imitative* ones, not as painting the object of the thought, but the situations, effects, the modifications of the soul,—and these I define

ANALOGOUS GESTURES.

These are partly founded on the tendency which the soul has to approximate itself to sensible ideas, and consequently to express itself by the imitative modifications of the form, until they acquire a due degree of *vivacity;* as, when one refuses assent to a position, one scatters it abroad (in idea) and, with a motion of the hand reversed, seems to put it aside.

Analogous gestures are likewise grounded on the force or influence with which certain ideas naturally operate upon *others*, upon the *communication* (if the phrase may be allowed me) which there is between the regions of clear and obscure ideas, which generally direct and modify each other by a reciprocity of action.

It is thus, for instance, that the series of ideas will determine a walk; whether the step shall become more tardy, or more rapid ; more firm, or more moderate ; in a word, more or less *uniform*. This walk is determinable by the series of *obscure* ideas which tacitly direct the will, and receive the laws of the *clear* ideas which govern it.

The influence of their several powers are reciprocal. For this reason, every situation of the soul, every interior movement, has its regular progression ; so that we may say of all characters, in general, that which the wife of Hercules says of Lychas,

His mind is like his walk.
Seneca, Trag. Herc. fur. Act ii. Sc. 2.

There are several other gestures which are kinds of involuntary phenomena ; these are really physical effects of interior movements of the mind ; but we only comprehend them as signs which nature has affixed by mysterious cords to

the secret passions of the soul; and for this reason, says a philosopher, that, in the common
affairs of civil life, one man may not be able
easily to impose upon *another*.   No one has
ever yet explained to us, in a satisfactory manner, why sad and sorrowful ideas operate on the
lachrymal glands, or why gay and cheerful ones
act upon the diaphragm ; why fear and anxiety
discolour the cheek, or why shame and modesty
tinge it with a deep and sudden crimson.   I shall
reunite all these phenomena under the head of

PHYSIOLOGICAL GESTURES.

I beseech you, in mercy to me, not to consider
this classification as arranged under the severe
laws of *logic :* it is the simple idea of a mere
observer, who solely seeks to establish some kind
of order amongst facts, the comparison and truth
of which must be refuted or confirmed by an
ulterior examination.

Amongst the *physiological* gestures, many will
be found which do not obey the arbitrary will
of the soul; she cannot *retain* them when sentiment commands : she cannot fail them when the
real sentiment does not exist.   The tears of
grief, the paleness of fear, and the blush of

shame or modesty are all of this involuntary kind.

As no one can have a right to expect impossibilities, we dispense with these involuntary variations in the comedian, and are perfectly satisfied if he gives us a faithful imitation of those which are voluntary. Even here, however, some prudence and judgment are requisite in the execution of his designs. The rage which tears the hair in a frightful manner, which throws the whole visage into the distortions of grimace, which pants till every muscle swells, and the blood gushes up to the extended eyes, —such a rage may, perhaps, be a true representation of nature, but is very, very *disgusting* in the imitation.

" O, it offends me to the soul, to hear a robustious periwig-pated fellow tear a passion to tatters, to very rags, to split the ears of the groundlings, who, for the most part, are capable of nothing but inexplicable dumb shows, and noise."—*Hamlet.*

Thus says Shakspeare, and thus speaks nature. Is it then necessary to become absolutely intolerable to the *ear* and the *eye* to affect the *heart ?*　There exists one sole mode of exciting the action of involuntary feelings, but this mode is not at the command of every one.　Quintilian mentions having seen actors who, after performing pathetic characters, wept and sobbed for a long time after they had laid aside their masks.

　" Vidi ego sæpè histriones atque comœdos, cum ex aliquo graviore actu personam deposuissent, flentes adhuc egredi."

And speaking of himself,·he assures us that he had often shed tears and turned pale in the course of his pleadings.

　" Ipse—frequenter ita motus sum, ut me non lacrymæ Solum deprehenderint sed *Pallor* et vero similis dolor."—*Instit.* l. vi. c. i.

The whole of the secret consists in an ardent imagination, which every artist ought both to possess and exercise in the strong and rapid reproduction of images.　He will thus *habituate* himself to penetrate entirely into the subject with which he is occupied.　Then, without our labour, without our exertion, they will in time act with all the energy of spontaneous affections.

Perhaps it would be even possible so to accustom the corporeal powers to the affections of the mind, by frequently repeated images, as to acquire an ascendancy in this difficult point. I have heard of actors who could fill their eyes with tears at a moment's warning. The weepers at funerals, who were paid by the ancients for shedding these drops of sorrow at the death of those for whom they could not have been the least interested, seems to confirm the practicability of this idea. Happy the actor who has acquired this talent, and knows how to produce it with propriety and effect! for experience proves that a *single tear*, discovered on the countenance of the speaker, often pleads more forcibly than fifty lines of complaining declamation!

It would be, nevertheless (according to my judgment), extremely dangerous to counsel an artist to heat his imagination on every occasion. Before the actor resigns himself to the government of his feelings, he ought to be sure that he shall retain the power of guiding and correcting them when they are growing too impetuous; for, as Shakspeare advises his actor,

" In the very torrent, tempest, and (as I may

say) whirlwind of your passion, you must acquire and beget a temperance, that may give it
smoothness."

There is no occasion to imitate the temerity
of the ancient actor who, in the part of ELECTRA,
brought on the urn which contained the ashes of
his own son.

But, as I have far exceeded the bounds of a
moderate letter, I shall resume my observations
at a future period.

LETTER VIII.

On perfect Inaction—The proud Man—The mild Man—The phlegmatic Man—Idleness and Vacancy—Lavater—An Actor ought to think for himself—Repose—Passage from Repose to Attention.

AMONG the different situations of the soul, which the body serves to express, we shall first consider that of *perfect inaction:* for this may, in some sense, be said to have its *peculiar expression;* I imagine that it would be useless to endeavour to define what I understand by *perfect inaction.*

We are aware that, in the most perfect equilibrium of the mind, the most profound repose of the passions, the soul still retains a certain portion of activity.

Represent to yourself a man who contemplates a tranquil scene of nature; not an enthusiastic admirer of her beauties, but one still and placid as nature seems herself at such an hour and in such a position.

Or suppose he is listening to some indifferent conversation of his friend or his neighbour, and you will not perceive any sensible trait of pleasure in him; no decided marks on his forehead, in his eye, or upon his lips; his aspect is neither curious, troubled, nor vacant; in a word, you find the whole man immovable; every thing seems in its right place, each trait in its perfect equilibrium, as in the drawing which Le Brun has made of *Repose*.

The whole of the countenance will be analogous to the situation of the soul. The attitude of the rest of the body, erect or seated, will not less indicate the quietude and inaction of the soul. The idle hands will repose themselves on the knees, in the pocket, in the frill of the shirt; a movement of the fingers, wandering without object, will still more betray the want of some occupation in the soul.

While the body is seated, the feet, equally devoid of action, cross themselves in a listless manner; one knee is reposed on the other; the body itself sometimes assumes an upright, and quickly relaxes into a bending posture; a heavy motion of the eyelids, such as that which precedes sleep, also demonstrates that all is numbed and quiet in the mental regions. Particular ideas, passions, and inclinations are predominant in each living soul: the shades and variations may be immense, while the *essence* is immutable and fixed. To explain my idea, let us examine a few attitudes.

The proud man *(Plate* III.) thrusting one hand into his bosom, carries it as high as he is able, and places the elbow of the other arm a-kimbo; his head is thrown a little backwards; his turned-out feet are at a distance from each other; he rests on one leg, while the other is thrown before it with extended dignity.

A *mild character* (I do not mean an effeminate one) carries the arms folded across the middle of the body; his head rests in a vertical position; it is neither thrown back, nor reposed on the breast; his steps are short; and his feet, though not *turned in,* are far from running into the opposite extreme.

The hands joined behind the back, and consequently removed from the active powers they possess in the contrary position, give ideas of much phlegm, and a perfect want of curiosity and attention. *(See Plate* IV.) The largeness of the belly, which sometimes makes the arms fall (naturally as it were) behind, might render this position more commodious, although one equally easy might take place here, to wit, that of propping the arms by the sides: the ex-

cess of fat naturally excites the suspicion of a
phlegmatic character.   When a vain man assumes this character, it is neither less speaking
nor less expressive *(see Plate* V).   Inattention and incuriosity have a strong resemblance
to pride ; and in such a position, the chest and
body are thrust more prominently forward, but
we do not remark in this figure, as in the *first,*
that the feet are rather turned in, or the head
resting on the chest.

One judges of a character with less certainty
from particular traits than when we contemplate
them combined together.   By the head, which,
not being properly placed on the neck, sinks
upon the bosom; the open lip, which draws
down the chin with its natural weight; the eyes
of which the pupils are almost obscured by the
lids ; the knees bending out, and the feet turned
in : all these marks present an attitude of which
the signification is remarkably striking *(as in
Plate* VI.)   One cannot avoid acknowledging a
soft soul and an idle mind, unsusceptible of any
attention, uninfluenced by any interest, which is
never thoroughly awake, and does not even possess the feeble energy which is necessary to give
the tension requisite for the muscles and for the
proper support of the members of his body.   An

attitude so full of nullity, so dead and inanimate, can only belong to the extremity of mournful imbecility, or the effects of the most contemptible idleness.

To fold the hands is a gesture of idleness, seen in those who are amused with sloth, and who maintain a drowsy league with sleep. The Egyptians, when they would exhibit an express character of laziness in their hieroglyphics, interlaced the arms : it is also an assumed gesture of meditation.

Lavater is a book which I have not ready at hand, and even if I had, I should not consult him very frequently. Strange notions, whose depth and value I have not thoroughly fathomed, might confound and perplex my own ideas. If you happen to have the book, I beseech you to read what is there said concerning attitudes.

This matter cannot easily be omitted, because I remember that the author there treats of the conclusions which may be drawn even from the hand writing of a man, in judging of his character, and of which he furnishes the proofs.

It is necessary that the comedian should judge, according to the *character* of his part, what attitude and deportment he should choose for scenes of tranquil dialogue. The best digested rules, the finest picture galleries in the world will not exempt him from the necessity of *thinking* for *himself*: for the choice and application of gestures exclusively belong to him ; and nature affords a variety which the most indefatigable observation is unable to exhaust. I ought, in the meantime, to add a remark on the subject of change from a *tranquil* to an *active* position. A man in the state of repose, when enticed and excited by any object to the display of his exterior activity, will discover his *intention* before the *action* is manifest to himself. He will have his hands, arms, feet, in short his whole frame in readiness to execute the first signal of the soul. The attitude most expressive of nonchalance, and most distant from activity, is when the body is seated at its ease, and leaning against any supporting object, the arms folded, and the legs crossed (*as in Plate* VII.).

Thus, the last moment of the tranquil attitude, I mean that approaching the nearest to coming activity, is the reraising the body directed towards the object which excites our interest, placing the hands equally separated upon the knees (*as in Plate* VIII.) ; and by these methods disposing the whole frame to exert itself and enter into immediate action.

If the motive of the action develope itself successively, the preparatives will follow the same progression : for example, the legs crossed, and the feet drawn behind, will separate themselves at once, and fix themselves at their place in a firm manner; the unfolding of the arms will ensue, &c.

This will have equal place, even when no exterior object provokes the activity ; when it is solely employed in considering attentively : we turn towards those we are speaking to, we advance near the object which interests us, in a manner which more or less announces the *intention* and predisposition to *enter* into a particular action.

LETTER IX.

Costume—Dancing—On Soliloquies, or Monologues—Sallust's Observations on Catiline's Mode of Walking—Hamlet—Lear—Tancred.

You are right when you say that in some of my delineations I abandon general traits, in attaching myself too much to the characteristic signs of *nations*, and the peculiar classes of *society*. The hands thrust into the clothes, or hid in the bosom, presuppose a certain kind of *costume;* as the feet, turned in and out, indicate the first elements of the modern art of *dancing*. I do not mean to give you finished drawings. If my *etchings* of the gestures and passions should offer you some general ideas of feelings and expressions, common to all ages and all nations, my end will be attained. We have just considered man in a state of *quietude*, let us now take him in the opposite point of view. He weighs his action and his position ; he examines the party it is most proper for him to take ; he searches out the most assured means of attaining his ends ; his memory recalls similar situations to his mind. In a word, he compares, discusses, and reasons. The expression will here be more or less animated, according to the cause which shall disclose his activity ; while the sole love of truth, which tranquilly searches for fresh sources of knowledge, developes the activity of the soul ; or whilst an agreeable play of the imagination is its employment : then, also, the expression will be more feeble, more moderate, and more cold ; than whilst the head, labouring for the interests of the heart, ought to consider and weigh the advantage of man ; his good, his evil, his happiness, and his misery.

When Hamlet appears in that situation so terrible and insupportable, where he argues both for and against the commission of *suicide*, he ought most surely to present an expression very different from that of a cold moralist, who reasons upon the same topic, not as an argument which comes home to his own bosom, but as a mere problem for the exercise of his faculties. Nevertheless, the love of truth is also capable of producing a very great interest in the mind. Pythagoras offered a hecatomb to the Muses when he had discovered the demonstration of the geometrical proposition which still bears his name.

The reflections and reasonings, which are ad
mitted on the theatre, are always divided in two
parts,—the sentiments of the heart, and the passions.

It is from these that *gesture* receives its more
particular modifications, the determinate degree
of warmth, the transition or the repose more or
less marked, &c.

Since it is impossible to develope all the various shades of interior activity, I shall confine
myself to some observations which may serve as
a model for a number of others of this kind.

It is principally against the rule of analogy,
almost every where observed in nature, that our
actors mostly offend. This offence occurs most
frequently in their *soliloquies* or *monologues*. Sallust, among the numerous characteristic traits of
Catiline, distinguishes his walk sometimes slow
and sometimes hurried.

" Animus impurus diis hominibusque infestus,
neque vigiliis, neque quietibus sedari poterat : ita
conscientia mentem excitatam vexarat, igitur
color ei exsanguis, foedi oculi, *citus modo, modo
tardus incessus,*" &*c*.

The historian attributes this irregularity to the

inquietude of his conscience, stained by so many crimes, and above all by that most abominable of all vices, assassination.

I have no objection to urge against this explanation ; nevertheless, it strikes me that the grand and perilous projects, which Cataline was meditating against his country, might have contributed, in an equal degree, to the production of these appearances !

Whilst the man developes his ideas with facility and without impediment, his walk is more unconstrained, more brisk, and continues in a more uniform manner.   When the series of ideas present themselves with difficulty, his step becomes more slow, more embarrassed ; and when, at length, a doubt of an important nature suggests itself to his mind, the man stops suddenly short (*See Plate* IX.).   In those situations where the soul hesitates between unequal ideas, and finds obstacles and difficulties on all sides, while she pursues each train of thoughts only to a certain point—passing rapidly from one suggestion to another—then the step grows irregular, hurried, and undetermined.

From hence the dubious pace in all the affections of the soul when *doubt* and an incertitude between jostling ideas take place : but above all in that terror which inwardly agitates and torments the conscience struggling in vain to deliver itself from the load.

The play of the hands is modified after the same manner as that of the walk—it is free, unconstrained, easy, and mobile, while the ideas develope themselves without any difficulty, and follow each other in a natural succession: It is inquiet and irregular, the hands are agitated, and move themselves without design, now towards the bosom, now towards the head, the arms fold and loosen, as the thought is arrested during his walk, or hurried into uncertain or strange tracks. The moment that a difficulty presents itself, the play of the hands entirely ceases—the eye, which, as well as the head, had a gentle and placid motion, while the thought was easy, and unfolded itself without labour, or wandered from one angle to the other, while the soul strayed from thought to thought, in this new situation looks straight forwards, and the load falls on the heart, until, after the first shock of doubt (if it be allowed me so to express myself) suspended activity resumes its former walk.

The sublime character of Hamlet (see Plate X.) offers a very strong example of this kind of change—a change of sentiment, which ought to display itself on the countenance of the actor who has studied his author with taste or precision. When the unhappy Prince has discovered the reasons which make self destruction so criminal a step—he exclaims " ay, there's the rub," and at the same moment should give the *exterior* sign of that which his *interior* penetration alone has enabled him to discover.

When the wretched Lear (*as exhibited in Plate* XI.) recollects the unworthy treatment he has experienced from his daughters, who, during the horrors of a tempestuous night, had exposed his gray locks to all the fury of the winter winds, he changes his tones, and suddenly exclaims " That way madness lies."

There does not really exist any exterior object from which this miserable father need avert his eyes with fear—yet, notwithstanding, he suddenly turns round from the spot where he had first been stationed, seeking as it were, with one hand reversed, to endeavour to push away this miserable and tormenting recollection.

Plate XII. represents Tancred, in Thompson's beautiful play of " Tancred and Sigismunda." Tancred, the heir of the Norman Kings, had been bred up under the care of Siffredi, Chancellor of Sicily.   His throne was usurped at that time by a tyrant, to whose daughter the rightful diadem of the Royal Orphan was bequeathed. Tancred, in the mean time, is supposed the son of a Baron of Apulia, an old friend and fellow warrior of Siffredi's. A strong attachment takes place between the young Prince and Sigismunda the daughter of his protector and benefactor. Siffredi, in the mean time, anxious for his charge, contrives an alliance between Constantia and Tancred, hoping by this expedient to unite the rival interests which had long distracted his country. The birth of Tancred is made known. A meeting takes place between him and Sigismunda. The generous prince, to silence her delicate objection, gives her a paper, to which his name is affixed, desiring her to present it to her father, with his commands that it should be filled up with a strict and solemn marriage contract. Siffredi, resolving to sacrifice his daughter's happiness to the interests of his country, has a promise of marriage from the King to Constantia substituted in its place, and reads it aloud, with the King's subscription, before the astonished Monarch and his whole applauding Council. Tancred retires in confusion; Siffredi follows. The King upbraids him; his protector urges him to become the father of his people; to sink the passions of the individual in that glorious appellation ; to conquer love, and sacrifice it to his honour.   The injured Tancred loudly exclaims,—" *Such honour I renounce with sovereign scorn—greatly detest it and its mean adviser.*" After this violent burst, the actor ought to make a movement of choler with his open hand, directing it to the feet of the venerable old man, to convey to him his contempt of the *nothingness* of the word *honour*, in the sense he had placed it. But you will often make similar observations to these of your own accord : those importunate and disagreeable ideas, which the mouth rejects, with the repetition of the word *Pho*, are in some measure likewise repulsed by a rapid agitation of the hand from one side to the other, as if we wished to chase away a teasing insect, which returns with double eagerness to the attack.

The extension of the right arm and hand is a gesture of various import ; it denotes protection, reproof, command, admonition, and invitation. Historians have taken notice of most of the expressions of the gesture of the hand.   Flavius Flaccus, made use of this warning gesture of the hand instead of speech ; for when Mutius began to call the tribes of the people to give their voices for the establishment of some new laws, propounded by Tiberius Gracchus in favour of the people, he could not proceed according to his accustomed order in the like case, for the great noise those behind made thrusting forward, and being driven back again.

In the meantime Flavius Flaccus, one of the Senators, got upon a place where all the people might see him, and when he found his voice could not be heard by Tiberius, he made a sign with his hand that he had matter of great importance to communicate. Tiberius understood this gesture of the hand, and bade them make a lane for him to pass through. Flavius came at length to him, and betrayed a conspiracy against him. This gesture is particularly expressive of command : Ovid observes " Quis nescit longas regibus esse manus."

Crinagoras, a Greek poet, praising Cæsar, says, " His right hand was mighty to command, which by its majestic power and authority, did quell the fierce and presumptuous audacity of barbarous men." Haydon has introduced this gesture very finely in his picture of the Judgment of Solomon, in the hand of the Monarch staying the division of the living child.

To put out the raised hand, and to shake it as it were into a shout, is the expression of those

who boast, triumph, and exultingly express the
raptures of their joy.   This gesture is grounded
in nature, and is common to all nations when
they are joyful.

When fine and important ideas present themselves, during the course of an examination, the
aspect acquires vivacity, the eyebrows are attracted towards the angles of the nose, the forehead is covered with wrinkles, and the eye itself,
that it may be better able to concentrate the
visual rays.   The same as when we are desirous
of examining an object of peculiar fineness, or
placed at a certain distance.   The sign, or index,
is then on the closed lips, as if the person thus
employed was fearful lest the hurry of the *less
important* thoughts should trouble the examination of the more *essential ideas*.   The gesture
perfectly accords with—*Peace ! Attend !* which
a man pronounces to himself, equally when he
encounters a doubt, or an object of importance.
Often, also, the object is placed between the eyebrows, on the wrinkles of the forehead, as if the
point to which the attention ought to be directed
was susceptible of being indicated or subjected.
This pantomime (which really comes to the assistance of thought) of remembrance, and inte-

rior examination, consists, if the phrase be allowed, of bottling up the senses, in covering the eyes, in veiling the face with the two hands. For interior operations execute themselves proportionably better as they are the less troubled by the exterior impressions of the senses.

For this reason, love, sorrow, and chagrin, as well as all the reflective passions, delight in the silence and obscurity of groves. The owl is the attribute of the Goddess of Wisdom, because an inhabitant of the deserts: he makes his watch in the stillness and obscurity of the night. There are other signs which accompany reflection; as, for example, the serene and clouded aspect, according to the freedom or restraint of the movement. There are motions in which the hand seems to come as an assistant to the head; as when, after too intense occupation, it is oppressed with the blood which mounts upwards in too great abundance. These sorts of actions are less important, and details on this head would, perhaps, be superfluous: besides, I have not promised you any thing more than fragments and light essays. You wish me to give you an explanation of what we mean by the *affections*; and, indeed, it is high time that this branch of my subject should be considered: it is the most important of all pantomimical exertion. As I know not when I may be able to comply with this requisition, I send you, in the meantime, a little book, which has fallen accidentally in my way, "A Lecture on Mimicry, 1777." If it give you no great instruction, it will at least serve to amuse you for some few vacant hours.

LETTER X.

On the Affections of the Soul—Of Desire—The different species of Smiles—Negation and Assent.

I do not feel myself at all inclined to consult the philosophers who have written on the affections of the soul.

I am well acquainted with the almost incredible diversity of their opinions, and it is more than probable that the confusion of their systems would involve me in a labyrinth from which I should find much difficulty in extricating myself; I shall therefore run the risk of making a classification for you, which seems more congenial to my proposed object. It will be indifferent whether any one has or has not made it before me.

I call by the term *affection* every strong activity of the soul which, by reason of its vivacity, is accompanied by a sensible degree of pleasure and of pain : I consequently distinguish two sorts of them; for this activity consists in the intuition of that which exists, or in the effort to obtain that which we *wish*. This last species is denominated *desire*, while in the first predicament we appear more passive——that is to say, we merely receive impressions. Desire, as we have hitherto explained it, is an effort, an interior tendency of the spirit, which frequently, of its own accord, and without any excitation or interest of the heart, feels a very lively interest, the sole end of which is to learn and to comprehend. The mind has then equally an affection of desire, which, from the origin of time, has worked miracles in noble souls, and urged them on to sacrifice more pleasures, and exert more corporeal energy, than any other incitation whatever. The mind has also its intuitive affections——for it arrests itself with satisfaction at that which is rich in ideas, well ordered, harmonious, or beautiful, without drawing any other advantage or profit from it, more than what the simple knowledge of things is capable of affording ; and it is with real sorrow that it observes the opposites of these affections ; to wit——that which is void of sense, ill-contrived, irregular, ugly, dissonant, &c. The affections of the heart have place when *self* is the object ; to wit——when we view a subject under the forms in which it is advantageous or hurtful to ourselves——when we love, when we hate ; in short, whenever we are desirous to unite with or to avoid any particular object. Those affections of the mind which display themselves in the countenance consist in admiration and in smiles. The smile is various, and capable of uniting and mixing itself with many of the other affections: there is, for example, an ironical and a sardonic smile. It is united to contempt in the first instance, and associated with hatred in the second. This affection, however, is capable of taking place, without any admixture of this nature; and genuine laughter consists in bursts of gaiety, while beholding harmless faults, strong contrasts, disproportions, and dissonances.

This is not the place for me to occupy myself in a research after the veritable source of ridicule.

The drawings of Le Brun and some others, on this head, partake to much of caricature; they are not worth the trouble of sending to you. Every one knows what it is to laugh, though there are some who do not know how to govern their mirth; and he whose visage is not adapted to laughter, will surely never acquire the science by rule and lessons. Descartes has already remarked, that some persons in weeping have a physiognomy similar to what others present when smiling: reverse the rule, and it will be found equally true. It is precisely because we so easily remark the various inflexions of this sort, and we find them ridiculous, that we have an exact idea of the gestures proper for laughter or for tears. In society we must take these inflexions as we find them, but are not forced to be equally complaisant when an imitation of them at a public theatre is the matter in debate. There are some men who cannot vary the traits of their faces, without offering us a disgusting appearance of the upper lip, or a wretched set of ugly teeth.

I would exhort the comedian to study not only the effect of the passions, but also their operations on his own face, that he may be able to distinguish those which become, as well as those which disfigure it. Indeed it would be wise to quit the stage entirely, where the first grand requisite, an expressive countenance, is wanting.

I dare say I might have spared myself the trouble of this advice for what is its utility, if in general the most part of men choose their situations haphazard, and become what they *are,* rather from blind predilection than a veritable penchant founded on real talents? This observation applies to the player in particular. A man truns player, or soldier, equally through *want* or *imprudence*—rarely by inclination, or by the true invocations of genius.

You will find more drawings than one on the subject of admiration in Le Brun. The first of these drawings is the most agreeable and the most exact. If you examine the traits with which the painter characterises this affection (a name which some, however, deny as belonging to admiration), you will remark that the body imitates the expansion of the soul, whilst seeking to seize on a grand object, with which all its representative forces appear to be replete. The mouth and eyes are open, the eyebrows are slightly drawn upwards, the arms are certainly nearer the body than in quick and animated desire, yet they are still somewhat extended; in other respects, the body and the traits of the countenance are in repose. Add yet to this the dilation of the chest, which we have already remarked, and which is a painting coincident with analogous expression, because admiration belongs to homogeneous expressions, and you will here perceive that all gestures may be considered as homogeneous and analogous. Thus you may explain the enlargement of the eye to be a gesture of the motive genus, or made by design;

for the soul would wish to attract from the object (which is here supposed to be large and visible) as many rays as possible. The immobile direction of the eye upon an object is also made by design, since it is solely through the medium of the eye that the mind can gratify its knowledge of the object—the extension of the arms can only take place at the first instant ; that is, when the soul is more eager to seize and retain an object in its power than when it already begins to taste the subsequent enjoyment. From the time this first moment of joy is past, the arms gently redescend, and come nearer to the body. It is otherwise in the case of gestures of admiration and sublimity, a variation which Le Brun has not remarked : for here the head and body are thrown a little back, the eye is open, the aspect elevated, and, by an image which coincides with the expression analogous to the sentiment, the whole figure of the man becomes straight : nevertheless, the feet, the hands, and the traits of the visage are in repose ; or if one hand is in movement, it is not held forth as in simple admiration, but lifted upwards *(as in Plate* XIII).

While extraordinary corporeal powers excite our admiration at that movement, an interior motion and inquietude agitate those parts of our own frame which are analogous. Astonishment, which is merely a superior degree of admiration, only differs from it in this respect: the traits which I have just pointed out become more characteristical; the mouth is more opened, the look more fixed, the eyebrows more elevated, and the respiration more difficultly retained. Astonishment, like thought, stops suddenly short when an object of interest presents itself unexpectedly to the view.

To throw up the hands to heaven is an expression of admiration, amazement, and astonishment, used by those who flatter and excessively praise. This expression always appears at some unexpected accident, and is used by painters to express amazement. This gesture was observed in a mother who had the misfortune to behold her son shot dead in Hart Street, Covent Garden. The elevation of the hand turned outward must always bespeak astonishment. This is finely expressed in Raffaelle's Cartoon of Paul and Barnabas at Lystra, by an old man lifting up the garment, and looking at the limb of one he remembered to have been a cripple.

A success unauthorized by our expectation, an event, or a thing, which takes place contrary

to the judgment or calculation we had previously
formed, excites admiration ; a sentiment which
generally manifests itself by a lightly scornful or
a bitter kind of smile, when the contrast between
the *thing itself* and the *idea* is to the disadvantage of the former.   A characteristic trait of this
sort of admiration is a kind of oscillation, or
shaking of the head, very difficult to be described
when its object is uninteresting, or when other
affections do not associate themselves with it.
This movement is different from the one with
which we reject or approve a thought, or which
serves for the expression of displeasure—it is
more slow, more uniform, more durable, less
hasty ; in short, it is that kind of shake of the
head you would yourself give, while I attempted
the definition, because you would not know how
to conciliate the explication with the fact.   It is
impossible for me to vindicate the veritable cause
of this expression.   I might perhaps supply it
by ingenious hypotheses—but this resource, no
doubt, would not please you, and you would look
on this expenditure of ingenuity as ill employed.
The shaking of the head in negation, and the
motion previous to assent, will perhaps be able
to explain themselves better.   The first seems,
in general, to indicate that one turns aside from

an idea which one rejects; and the second, that one *approaches* or *accedes* to it. A metaphor expressed with so much native perspicuity, by the Greek and Latin words,

Προσνευω—απονευω

Adnuo—abnuo

that *Nigidius,* without giving their explication, quotes them as words of extraordinary significance.

Quum adnuimus et abnuimus motus quidem ille vel capitis vel oculorum a natura rei quam significat, non abhorret.—*Gellius.*

This serves to explain why, in a proposition, to the truth of which we are ready to acquiesce, we carry the head, at various returns, towards the speaker, and that we draw it back, on the contrary, where the opinion delivered does not coincide with our own sentiments; a direction which the *eyes* also commonly obey.

I will not employ myself any longer on the subject of admiration, nor of the various affections of the mind in general, seeing that they almost universally unite themselves to those of the heart, although these latter are the most strong: so much is this the case that the ex-

pression of the first so closely confounds itself
with the last that it is extremely hard to comprehend their different shades.   In my next letter I shall treat of the gesture proper to this
more interesting species of affections; that is,
where the representation of the object does not
exclusively occupy our thought—but where the
ideas of ourselves, of our advantages, or our
wants, associate themselves in a manner more or
less interesting.

LETTER XI.

The Tragedy of King John—Aversion and Desire—Rous-
seau's Sophia—Devotion—De Montfort—The Reply of
Cain after the Murder of his Brother—The Hero and the
Philosopher.

In Shakspeare's tragedy of *King John, Hubert*
relates to his master the manner in which his
subjects are affected by the death of *Prince*
Arthur, and that this event, as well as the des-
cent of a powerful body of French, formed the
subject of every one's conversation.

> I saw a smith stand with his hammer, thus,
> The whilst his iron did on the anvil cool,
> With open mouth swallowing a tailor's news;
> Who, with his shears and measure in his hand,
> Standing on slippers (which his nimble haste
> Had falsely thrust upon contráry feet),
> Told of a many thousand warlike French,
> That were embatteled and rank'd in Kent:
> Another lean, unwash'd artificer
> Cuts off his tale, and talks of Arthur's death.
> > *Shakspeare.*

The immobility of the blacksmith, who preserves the attitude he was in at the moment

when struck with wonder, is a trait as expressive as it is natural : all the intellectual faculties are chained by a single object : no one thought foreign to the subject rests in the soul : no— not even an arbitrary change of position in the body. Consequently, the man struck with sudden astonishment ought to remain fixed like a statue to his posture for the time. *(See Plate* XIV.)

What species of affection we first consider is perfectly indifferent ; the desire which demands that the thing should change its situation, or the contemplation which examines its actually existing state.

The moral philosophers oppose aversion to desire ; but, following the general sense which I have attached to this word, aversion also belongs to the class of the desires, because it tends to change a present situation into a better. We have then *two* sorts of desires : one which strives to attain good, the other which endeavours to avoid evil. This last desire again subdivides itself; since we either desire to remove ourselves from evil, or to get rid of it : we think then of flight or of attack. Since, in all these cases, expression offers very sensible differences, we ought to establish three kinds of desires ; one tends towards enjoyment, the other withdraws itself for safety, and the third approaches anew, to put to flight or destroy the hurtful object. That all these desires are susceptible of infinitely varied modifications is self-evident.

One of the modifications of desire, most worthy of observation, is that of the man who feels an uncomfortableness, a privation, a secret uneasiness, without being able to discover the reason; or, to speak more properly, when a man is tormented by a violent desire, without being conscious of its object. Such is the situation of Sophia, in Emilius and Sophia, by Rousseau: the artless girl is uneasy—restless—she is in love— with whom?—she knows not: pressed on the subject, she avows Telemachus (a being of fiction) as the object of a devouring flame which consumes her, and to which she can neither attribute name nor origin.

This imaginary malady is well known, yet baffles all the skill of Æsculapius.

The man in this predicament moves from place to place, from side to side; he turns himself in all possible directions; his hands are constantly rubbing one against the other—or, stretched forward without a determinate design, seize and grasp the first object that comes in their way;

his gait is interrupted and varied into every possible direction : in a word, he makes a thousand movements, not one of which continues any length of time, not one indicates a decided position. We simply perceive, in his general motions, that he is agitated by some violent desire, and that he seeks to avoid some misfortune with which he conceives himself menaced, or that he wishes to wreak his resentment and fury on some object or other.

A different modification on the part of the object is that which we either desire or hold in abhorrence—to which we would unite, or from which we would separate ourselves : it is a certain *je ne sais quoi*, inherent in ourselves, and which leaves in us either a pleasant or a disagreeable sensation.

Under such circumstances the action of gesture has also its characteristical marks : whilst a man of piety endeavours to arrive at a perfect and mystical union with the divinity, he paints by his gestures, his mien, and his motions that complete retirement and detachment from earthly concerns, which always precede these efforts of a devout heart : his joined hands are retired and clasped towards the upper part of his chest ; the elbows jetting out will be carried forwards, pro-

portioned to the force of the devotion ; the apple
of the eye, directed towards Heaven, will hide
itself under the eyelid, and the remainder of the
ball will plainly be visible *(as in Plate* XV).

The wretch tormented by a racking and insupportable idea seeks to deliver himself from it
by all manner of dissipations : his gait is as vague
and as uncertain as his countenance.   He is perpetually varying his attitudes, and he keeps continually rubbing his forehead, as if he wished to
efface from his memory the last trace of the
thought which thus afflicts him.

Such is the situation of the unhappy De
Montfort, in the play of the ingenius lady who
has favoured the public with the plays on the
passions.

While on this subject, I would wish to recom-
mend the perusal of this lady's excellent dramas
to every lady and gentleman of the theatres, desirous to improve themselves in the art which
they profess.   In this painful state, the man tormented by his own conscience is the object of
self violence ; he is fearful and trembling ; a leaf
falling, a zephyr whispering fills him with terror,
and inclines him to flight.

The answer of Cain, " Am I my brother's
keeper ?" certainly carries with it an air of effron-

tery and boldness: but who does not recognise, with the first glance, that this answer of Cain's is dissembled and false. If any one had this passage to recite, he would assuredly express with a trembling voice that fear which seeks to mask itself even by its very words.

A third modification is that where the object is truly out of the man, but also out of the dominion of the senses; the possession of which cannot be procured by the free will of any visible being; and consequently no exterior or determinate object can be employed for its attainment. Such, for example, is a passion for that kind of glory which only consists in the opinion which men form of our perfections, and which we can neither snatch by force, nor obtain by submission.

If the means of obtaining such objects are exterior, and act upon the senses, then, by affinity to the art of which we are treating, the desire which pursues them resembles that which has a sensible and exterior object for its aim: but if these means are not in the dominion of the senses, the person will be tormented by a desire which will make interior efforts; on which I have endeavoured to make an essay in a precedent letter.

The hero and the thinking man, both governed by ambition, are able to conceive this idea:
the first, to obtain an imaginary good, avails
himself of sensible objects; he precipitates himself amid crowds of combatants; he mounts the
scaling ladder, he snatches the colours of the enemy, and, like a madman, overturns every thing
which comes in his way or opposes his passage.

The thinking man does not stretch the muscles of his body, but the muscles of the soul; all
that he seeks to possess, or to get rid of, is in
himself and in his own brain; he pursues his
ideas, and searches for new sources of knowledge.

LETTER XII.

Of the Effects of Aversion and Desire—Anecdote of Tiberius,
from Suetonius—Example from the Tragedy of Merope—
On the Dress of Female Performers—Media and Jason—
Apollo and Niobe.

THE oblique position of the body is the first and
general trait of the play of all the desires which
carries them towards an object exterior and determinate.

Desire tends towards the object, whether it
be to possess or to attack it ; then the head, the
chest, and the superior part of the body in general throw themselves forward ; not merely because man, putting these parts in motion with
the greater facility, makes use of them first to
satisfy himself, but also because the feet are
forced to follow the rest of the body with more
celerity in this attitude : whilst aversion or fear
lead us to repulse the object, then the body
throws itself far back before the feet are in motion.

In strong and unforeseen affections this is

sometimes effected with so much precipitation and vivacity that the man, losing his equilibrium, if he does not quite fall down, at least makes some false steps.

The hypocrite Tiberius, an enemy to every species of adulation, one day retired backwards with so much precipitation, whilst a senator demanded pardon (for God knows what fault), that he tumbled to the ground.

" Adulationes adeo adversatus est, ut neminem senatorum aut officii, aut negotii causa, ad lecticum suám admiserit, consularem vero satisfacientem sibi ac per genua orare conantem, ita suffugerit ut caderet supinus."—*Sueton. in Tiber.* 627.

A second observation, which will be confirmed by the developement of each lively and animated desire, is, that the body constantly follows the *right* line in approaching or removing itself from the object. The reason of this is obvious, since desire urges us to unite or separate from the object as much as possible, and of all the lines drawn from one point to the other, the right line is the shortest; it follows then that the man, fixing his eyes upon the object of his desires, perceives nothing of all that separates him from it, and prefers pushing through the crowd, and opening a way with his elbows stiffened and thrust out, to taking a route less encumbered but more distant, which, by a slight circumbendibus, would conduct him with less pains and difficulty to his mark.

The son of Merope, in the tragedy of that name, wishing to avenge the death of his father on the tyrant Polyphontes, and to prevent his marriage with his mother, rushes through the guards, the populace, and the priests, till he reaches the victim he is eager to immolate. The same thing takes place in extreme terror: the man, without returning, carries the foot backward; and, staggering, thus makes several steps of flight in the same straight direction: above all, while he strives not to lose sight of the object which alarms him, that he may be able to judge of his danger, and direct his flight accordingly.

Something of this kind may be conceived by any one who has seen the drama of the Castle Spectre! The villain Osmond rushes into a chamber after a terrific dream, imagining himself to be yet haunted by the spectre which had tormented him in his broken and feverish slum-

bers.   He staggers, sinks into the arms of his
attendants; and ought, when he recovers, to retreat from some object present to his mental eye,
which inspires him with terror, and from which
he is all anxiety to remove himself.

In similar cases our actresses often are deficient in expression; because their long trains and
sweeping robes expose them to the danger of
falling in an indelicate manner : hurried on,
sometimes, by the real sentiment of the passion
which ought to be expressed, they suddenly start
back and, their feet entangling in the folds of
their ample drapery, they frequently find themselves obliged, in the most interesting situations,
to have recourse to their hands, to repair the
awkward disorder of their garments.

I am partial to all that can add ornament to
female dress, especially in a woman to whom
nature has not been unkind; I am still more
partial to a costume which is *exact* and rigidly
observed; notwithstanding all this, a truth of
expression is the most indispensably essential
rule of the art; and I cannot admit of any exception in this respect.   I should desire then, in
each part of sentiment, that the actresses should
employ all that inventive genius with which
they so well know how to vary their attire, and

with constant elegance, to arrange their sweeping robes in such a manner that they may not
be awkward or incommodious to them in the
developement of any passion which the scene
may chance to demand.   I cannot precisely
point out the most simple method of obviating
this difficulty, without doing an essential injury
to the general laws of costume ; but I am sure
that a very good effect would follow, if it could
be possible to obviate this cause of embarrassment to our actresses, and that their own per-
formances would be heightened in their effect,
as well as the general satisfaction of the spectators.

A third observation, which I have to make on
the play of the desires in general, concerns the
change occasioned by the positions and determinate connexions between the object of desire
or aversion and the persons inspired with them.
Ought I to impute the obscure manner in which
I explain my opinion on this head to myself or
to my subject ? Some examples taken from each
species of desires will perhaps render it more
plain.

First of all, my friend, let us suppose an object
of desire placed more high than the person desir-

ous of obtaining it ; or, what comes to the same point, that the personages are not of an equal height.

Whilst the little boy is desirous of springing up into the lap of his mother, he raises himself on his toes, stretching out his whole body ; every muscle is stretched, while his head falls a little back—his arms are elevated in the air. When the mother wishes to embrace the child, she bends down the upper part of her body, and perhaps the knees, letting the arms fall in such a way as to invite the child to precipitate itself into them. *(See Plate* XVI.)

In the desire of vengeance there ought to be a sensible difference between Jason, for instance, and Medea, while she rides, air-borne, in her car and murders his children before the eyes of the father,—Jason, in an agony, lays his hand on his sword—she, placed in security above his threats, throws down the reeking dagger, and pronounces these terrible words, " Go, bury them."

These are the very words of Euripides ; they are applied, however, to Creusa, and carry with them an augmented bitterness.

Στειχε προς οιχης καὶ θαπτε αλοχον.
Act v. *ver.* 1394.

It is a remark made somewhere else, that the movements of desire, in warding off an evil, are different according to the parts of the body we are willing to defend : he who is afraid of being crushed by the fall of a house, flies, urged onwards by the desire of self preservation, with his head bent and covered with his hands ; on the contrary, he who is menaced with the thrust of a sword covers his heart.

Represent to yourself an *Apollo* borne on a cloud, and prepared to pierce the bosom of one of the children of Niobe with a mortal arrow.

From the reunion of these two attitudes a third will be the result.

The head and the whole of the body will be thrown upwards, because the danger comes from above ; the look, suppliant with fear, is turned towards the God; and the bosom will be covered with the hands, *(as in Plate* XVII).

I could multiply observations of this nature to an infinite number : when we dread too sudden or violent a break on the optic nerve, by lightning or by any hideous object, or unpleasant and disgusting form, we shut the eyes or cover them with the hands. He who fears the noise of thunder, the effect of a shrill sound, or any other disagreeable tone, or impious or blasphemous discourse, stops his ears, turning the head at the same time; whilst he who can neither support the effects of either thunder or lightning, thrusts his head under the bed clothes, to avoid the disagreeable sensations of two distinct organs : on the other side, the man who strives to avoid a danger which is very near, for instance, that of being bit by a venomous serpent ready to fly at him, will save himself with his feet greatly elevated from the ground : whilst he who, hopeless of saving himself, sees danger hovering over his head, trembling, contracts his whole body, like the poor little bird which, when it beholds the vulture fending the regions of air above him, darts perpendicularly downwards to the ground.

It is thus that circumstances differently modified will vary the play of the desires in the developement of the means to attain the object of one's wishes, or to free oneself from the motives of our dislikes, to an almost incredible variety.

In running over all the observations I have made to the present period, I do not find an instance where the three kinds of desires are

united together : perhaps they will be found
hereafter, when we shall examine each species
separately. Since the order followed in our researches is a matter of no great moment, we
shall commence with the desire which inclines us
to approach near to our object.

LETTER XIII.

Violent and feeble Desires—Difference of Desire between a hard Drinker and a Bon Vivant—The Motive or Gesture, made with Design—The Curious Man and the Lover— The Beggar.

It is evident that the variety we remark in the play of desire, which carries us towards our object, of which I made mention in the last paragraph of my precedent letter, is founded upon the different analogies between the object desired and the person desiring. One of the most general rules of this play of gesture is, that the organ destined to seize on an object constantly tries to approach that object; for instance, he who listens advances the *ear ;* the savage who tracks his prey by the scent advances his *nose* as he proceeds; and when the object can be seized by the sense which is proper to this expression, it is the hands that are advanced, though in effect they are never perfectly idle in the expression of desire, however faint; and in these cases they are always open and stretched in a direct line, with the fingers spread out, whilst in the act of receiving; and shut, with the *palms* turned towards the ground, when in the act of seizing or drawing any thing towards us by force.

The gait is firm and lively, without being so heavy and impetuous as it is in choler. The physiological movements join themselves to these motives or actions without design : that is to say, that all the interior powers of man tend in a certain way to the exterior.

The eyes are more or less brilliant, the muscles are possessed of more or less activity, the cheeks are more or less coloured, the step is slow or hurried, the arms and legs are extended with more or less moderation ; the body gets rid more or less of its weight ; for, as I have already remarked, violent desire makes us start forward even to the point of falling down; whilst feeble desire only inclines towards its object in a gentle and hardly perceptible motion.

That which is the most remarkable in this play of desire is the synenergy of the powers, that is to say, their general rousing, even while the soul collects them together, for a service

which an individual would be capable of performing. It is not the same thing with pure
and disengaged contemplation, as with every
other desire of the soul. For here the soul
seems in some sort to lull to slumber those
other energies, to enjoy the unmixed delight of
that sensation which occupies it for the moment, and is so delightful to it. The better to
comprehend this difference, let us take for example the hard drinker consumed by a burning
thirst, and the voluptuous wine lover : the one
wishes to satisfy a pressing want, the other
seeks to administer agreeably to his palate.
Meantime, if you are desirous of a strong and
full expression, do not choose your examples
from those who have been educated in the
principles of what is termed, *savoir vivre*, or
beau monde ; an education of this kind teaches
a man the art of dissembling in a double way :
it gives him the power of hiding the real power
of his sentiments, in attributing to them one
which he does not possess. All the strong expressions of inclinations or personal tendencies,
and all weak expressions of the social affections
wound the *bon ton*, however true and proper in
other respects to places, to persons, and to cir-

cumstances; for this reason, the first are depressed below reality, and the last are carried
beyond truth.   The vulgar, the child, the savage,
in a word, the uncultivated man, are the true
models we ought to examine for the expression
of the passions, while we do not seek for beauty,
but merely for truth and force.

You will find, then, the voluptuous drinker
(Plate XVIII.) concentre in himself: his step
is short; the movement of the hand, which is
at liberty, is gentle ; the muscles of it are not
stretched, but it is generally fixed under the
other, which supports the glass. His eyes are
small (but do not, nevertheless, possess that arch
and fine look which we remark in the connoisseur who tastes his wine to judge of its quality).
They are often entirely shut, and even with firmness.   His head is sunk between his shoulders.
In short, the whole man seems to be absorbed in
the single sensation which agreeably tickles his
palate.   What a difference between the head
of a wine drinker and the thirsty drunkard.
In the latter, all his senses seem absorbed in
the desire which consumes him.   His haggard
eyes come out of his head; his steps are wide
and straggling; his body with his stretched out

neck bent forwards; his hands tightly clasp the cup, or are stretched out with eagerness to seize it: his respiration is rapid and uneven; and, in the case of his springing forwards to lay hold of the glass, his mouth is open, and his dry tongue appears through his lips, eagerly lapping the liquor on the surface of the vessel which contains it *(as in Plate* XIX). You think that I am here describing the highest degree of thirst, the " *anhelam sitim,*" as Lucretius calls it; but what you see here in its violence you will find, in a certain degree, in drought of a more moderate kind.

Let us consider, if you please, an example more noble than that of the wine drinker. Represent to yourself the interesting Juliet, who, awaiting her dear Romeo, exclaims:—" Hist! Romeo," &c. What, according to your opinion, ought to be her attitude? Without doubt her ear and all her body (though still and quiet, the better to distinguish the noise she hears) should be inclined to the spot where she expects the entrance of the personage. It is only on that side that the foot will be planted with firmness, while the other, rested on the point, will seem suspended in the air: all the rest of the body will be in a state of activity *(as represented in Plate* XX). The eye will be very open, as if to collect a great number of visual rays, for the object which does not yet appear to it. The hand will be directed to the ear, as if it could really seize the sound. The other arm, to preserve the equilibrium of the body, will be directed towards the ground, with the palm turned downwards, as if eager to push aside every intrusion which might trouble the attention requisite for a moment so replete with interest.

Although an object be foreign to the organs of sight and feeling, and only adapted to the sense of hearing, the eye, notwithstanding, will feel an eagerness to behold, the hands will make an endeavour to arrest it, and the whole body will tend to the encounter.

Take the opposite case, when one listens to distant and agreeable music, less to appreciate its value than to enjoy its effect. Here the person who listens will keep himself still, with his arms across, or reduced to inaction in a different attitude. His feet will be approaching each other; the tranquil eye will be feebly open or quite closed; the hand, and perhaps the body, will follow the heart with a slight movement. In this case the activity of the other senses will be equally deadened, as much as the circumstances will permit, that the whole attention of the soul may be able to indulge in the voluptuous enjoyment with which it is so agreeably affected.

I return to the motive, or gesture made with design, which I have spoken of before. Taken in its original sense, it does not really belong but to those desires which are chiefly directed towards sensible, exterior objects; but this gesture is sometimes also metaphorically employed; as, for example, in the communication of ideas, moral sentiments, volitions of the mind, &c. &c. The curious man and the lover, both demand the news of the day, or an avowal of return to the tender passion, with the body curved, and the hand open. In the same manner the beggar asks for alms, and the starved objects demand nourishment.

By an attentive observation you will find a great number of these metaphorical applications of the gesture motive to things purely intellectual: represent to yourself a man highly attached to the recital he is making, and who claims the attention of an auditor equally curious, equally interested in the circumstance, and you will find that the one and the other will lay hold of the hand, the arm, the coat, and the button, to attract or rouse each other reciprocally at those moments when attention flags and languishes; just as one would act in drawing a mobile object, or to put the arrested powers of a machine in motion. An instance of this occurs in Hubert's celebrated speech (quoted above) in King John, where he describes the Smith listening to the Tailor. Besides, the gesture of desire, directed by the sentiments or resolution of a free being, distinguishes itself from the expression of desire in a *passive* one; for, in the first case, the moral means commonly associate themselves to the physical. The gestures are full of motives which, according to the difference of characters, and the reciprocal connexions of persons, sometimes manifest themselves by humble regards and attitudes which soothe and flatter pride—sometimes by the amicable caresses which are so pleasing to good temper. These motives, also, often develope themselves by those simple, mild, and engaging regards which dispose the soul to softness and sympathy; by looks fierce and menacing which inspire a sense of fear; or by looks of a disagreeable nature, which provoke disgust and ennui. Pleasure prevails in one case, displeasure in the other: to the first instance one accords the thing desired as a recompense for agreeable sensation; and in the second, to escape from perceptions still more unpleasant.

LETTER XIV.

Of a Man bit by an Adder—Of Noxious Vapours—Opinion of a Philosopher—Of Le Brun—A Man alarmed at a Thunder Storm—Laocoon and the Serpent—Of Terror and Astonishment—The Synenergy of the Faculties—Trembling —Change of Colour—Medea—Of Astonishment—Error an Evil of the Mind—Concerning Figurative Expression —Affirmation and Negation—The Employment of Pride and Flattery in Different Persons.

THE rule which subsists with respect to the desire which carries us towards an agreeable object agrees equally well with that which removes us from an unpleasant one. *(This is exemplified in Plates* XXI. *and* XXII.) For the part of the body which suffers most, or is most menaced with the expectation of suffering, will be the first to withdraw or turn aside. The idea of the design by Lairesse, of a man already bit by a serpent, or fearing so to be, is a false one. In flying away he still keeps his foot near the reptile; instead of which he ought to have drawn it away from the menaced danger with the same energy that one snatches the finger from the fire. In the former letter I have given some examples

applicable to this rule.   I shall here confine myself to the mention of a single one, which appears to me worthy of observation.   It relates to
the different shades of the expression of aversion,
as far as it relates to the senses of taste and
smell.   The movements of the nose and the lip,
which the intimate connexion of these two desires renders so similar, manifests in each of these
cases the wish to withdraw—occupies a *determinate place;* for example, whilst noxious vapours fill the atmosphere, the man then flies
away from the determinate place.   The attitude
and direction of flight have been already detailed
above.

In all cases where the nature of the evil is not
perfectly known on its first approach, and the
organs adapted to comprehending the knowledge
are not directly excited (as in the case of thunder,
for instance), then the desire of examining the
qualities, the proximity, and the greatness of the
evil associates itself to that of self preservation.
In short, in all cases where there does not exist
a total impossibility of avoiding or removing the
danger, a second but more *weak* desire is superadded to the first, to wit, that of repulsing the
evil, and of fortifying ourselves against it by our
own internal resources.   Nature will point out

the means best adapted for this, according to the circumstances which occur.   He who wishes to dissipate offensive smells puffs out his breath from his lungs with force, or beats about the air with an agitated hand.   Thus he who trembles at the unexpected attack of an enemy, in the moment of fear, opposes him with his two reverse hands.   The first of these concomitant desires has a great share in the expressions of fright and terror, which manifest themselves on the countenance.   For it makes the eyes spread and extend, the better to recognise the object by which it is menaced.   And the mouth too, if we may believe an English Philosopher, who speaks thus :—

" The reason why the eyes and mouth are suddenly opened in frights seems to be, that the object of danger may better be seen and avoided, as if Nature intended to lay open all the inlets to the senses, for the safety of the animal : the *eyes*, that they may see their danger, and the *mouth*, which is in this case an assistant to the ears, that they may hear it.   This may, perhaps, surprise some, that the mouth should be necessary to hear by ; but it is a common thing to see men, whose hearing is not very good, open their mouths with attention when they listen, and it is some help to them. The reason is, that there is a passage from the *meatus auditorius,* which opens into the mouth. Thus we see how ready Nature is, upon any emergency, to lay hold of every occasion for self preservation."— *Philos. Transact.*

Others hold opinion with Le Brun, that this opening of the mouth is occasioned by the emotions of the heart, whose palpitation raises a difficulty of breathing. It little matters to which of these two explications you give the preference; nevertheless, the former seems to have the advantage, inasmuch as it reduces the two phenomena to one common principle; and for this cause it is most acceptable to me. For, I could wish that all the obscure gestures attributed to physiology were placed in the more plain class of gestures motive. For the rest, it suffices to know that the tendency to inquire into and judge of the nature of the danger almost constantly associate, by very sensible reasons, to the desire of preservation in the individual, and that the action lasts, even after the man has turned his back and is flying with his hands before him.

If the dangerous object is visible, the fugitive turns back his head as he runs, and directs the ear to the place, if its approach can only then be distinguished by that sense.

A great painter, therefore, has done well in making his figures look back, under the impression of fear. I have seen one figure, however, that of a man alarmed at thunder, where, I think, Nature points out a different expression. He should not (in my opinion) turn round his face, but rather shut his eyes, covering them at the same time with one hand, and with the other stretched behind him, as if he wished to ward off the dreaded stroke. *(See Plate* **XXIII.**)

The second desire, *i. e.* of repulsing or removing the evil, which commonly unites itself to the wish of preservation, manifests itself during its presence, and as long as the terror, not having entirely overpowered the energies of the man, leaves any activity to his muscles. This is peculiarly remarkable when any obstacles are opposed to the fugitive, or when the peril is so near as that which menaced Laocoon from the serpents, who

> —Simul manibus tendit divellere nodos
> Perfusas sanie vitas atroque veneno,
> Clamores simul horrendos ad sidera tollit.

In the first moment of fear we stagger backward, or because we know not the degree of the peril, from its bursting unexpectedly upon us, we know not how to act, whether to fly or to defend ourselves. It seems to me that fear, in the first instance, where this denomination is most proper for it, is often an admixture of astonishment, fright, and anger ; at least somewhat of these three affections may be traced in it.

Terror makes us start back, renders us immovable, and discolours the cheek; astonishment makes us motionless for a moment, in the same attitude. Both of these open the eyes and mouth beyond their general proportions; anger makes us impetuously present the hand, as it were to meet the danger. In truth, this last gesture does not always take place; for, when the peril is instantaneous and with superior strength, the desire of self conservation makes the arms rise aloft, as if rather eager to demand assistance from above than seeking to repulse the evil in stiffening the frame against the attack. Of all the affections of the mind this is assuredly the most dangerous one for the health; and it seems to me that its ravages are sufficiently explained by the instantaneous combat of opposing and diverse passions, which succeed and mix with violence and rapidity.

You ask me in your last letter, if the remark concerning the synenergy of the faculties, which takes place in the desire of enjoyment, ought not to be equally applied to fear, to anger, and, in a word, to every species of desire. The little I am now about to say will furnish you with an answer to this question.

The gesture will be more or less modified by one or the other concomitant desire: sometimes the man will seek to know the nature of the peril with greater certainty; sometimes he will confine himself to the mere removing it from him. Le Brun cites a case where the whole body seems to concentrate, but he does not say a single word concerning the eyes or the lips, which ought to participate in that general contraction. There are, however, some cases which offer a similar phenomenon to that of the desire of enjoyment. For example, whilst the evil affects only one sense, while it is known, and the means of avoiding it is not the question, then the participation of the other senses sometimes manifest themselves: a bad smell makes not only the two organs affected close themselves, viz. the nose and the mouth, but the eyes also;

when the disgust acquires a greater degree of intensity. Nevertheless, it might be objected against this observation, that in the first movements the contraction and wrinkling of the muscles of the face are already sufficiently strong to diminish the opening of the eyes also. The remark, then, would be more striking if one said that one reenters into oneself, that one draws back each member, and as much as possible shuts up all the senses, when fear (as in the imminent danger of falling from a vast height) has amounted to such a pitch that one dreads to appreciate the peril, and has lost all hope of preservation. " I shall shut my eyes," says a man in a comedy, " that I may not be a witness of my own deplorable end."

The physiological phenomena caused by fear, whilst all the movements of human nature and, above all, the desire of self preservation find themselves interested, are so known, and their imitation so difficult for the actor that I think I ought to pass them over in silence. The icy seizure and the trembling of the limbs are easily imitated ; but the changes of colour, those signs of an imagination strongly depicted, are not to be copied by a mere cold intention.

Let us then quit this subject, that we may

enter on that of motive gesture, of which we have spoken above.

You well know that, to speak properly, one cannot retreat from the approach of evil, nor oppose resistance to it by holding out the hands, unless the object be really present and has a determinate place : notwithstanding we *do* retreat or throw back the body when we are fearful of hearing bad news.   Our own proper thoughts sometimes urge this effect, when our heart and our conscience reject any ideas as base, unworthy, or criminal.

Whilst *Medea*, transported with rage, consults with herself on the way in which she may inflict the most sensible wound on the heart of her perfidious Jason, and distracted by the desire of vengeance, forms this wish, " Ah! why has he not children by Creusa ?" or while she makes this still more terrible question, " Is he not already a father ?"   Then, with averted face, she holds forth her hands and throws back her body, whilst revolted nature makes her breathe a sudden cry from the bottom of her heart.   *(See Plate* XXIV.)

" Shocking thought, it freezes me with fear."

It is thus that a man generally starts back from a fearful idea, after it has acquired any degree of vivacity, as at the approach of any present evil with which his senses are struck, whether his soul has conceived this idea of its own accord, or it has been communicated to him by some other person.

The same thing happens in *astonishment*, whilst surprising and incredible ideas take possession of the soul as if it were by force.

It is thus, for example, that we expose ourselves to being ridiculous by too much credulity. It is for this reason that we remove, for a moment, from the person who recounts incredible things to us, though they may be in other respects perfectly indifferent to our well being; and that one turns aside at the recital of some *paradox*. It is thus, also, that the sudden appearance of a friend long thought dead, or at a great distance from us, makes us recede with fear, as if a spectre presented itself to our eyes.

It is useless to remark that in such situations one is equally occupied to appreciate and reconnoitre the danger of being deceived. We compare, for example, the friend we review with the image we had retained of him in our minds, to confirm the reality of his presence; we consider, with a fixed eye, and sometimes with a slight smile, the man who is telling us some story, or else examine him with a severe or contemptuous look, to be able to determine, by the play of his physiognomy, whether he is jesting or speaking seriously; and to satisfy ourselves concerning the way in which he will sustain this look, or how he will answer it by his mien and his words.

It would be here very easy for me to multiply the examples of such *figurative expressions:* an animated, lively negation, a refusal suddenly given with somewhat of humour, are always accompanied with a movement of the head and hands, as if we wished to scatter or push away the question or the prayer that is addressed to us.

On the contrary, when we affirm any thing with vivacity, or grant a favour with a good will, we employ an open hand, with the palm aloft, as if we wished to present it to the speaker, or to receive his: and this double disposition is only the figurative representation of the agreement of the judgment and the wits.

The gesture of aversion, as applied to moral objects, appears to me still more worthy of re-

mark; for you should have observed that the
expression of contempt assumes spontaneously
a trait of disgust; for example, the sight or recital of despicable actions, of base flattery, of
pusillanimous supplication, of servile weakness
in putting up with gross injuries, makes the
nose contract as if in the act of being hurt
by the smell of something disagreeable to its
nerves; and sometimes, when the contempt is
carried to a high degree, it is shown by a kind
of spitting, and manifested by the exclamation
of " Fie!"—which indicates a kind of wish to
purge the mouth from some putrid or pestilen-
tial substance.

Some other evils are more material, and merit
all our attention and observance. We tremble
because we compare their greatness with our
own littleness, their force with our proper weakness; we fly from a disgusting object on account
of the idea which we form of the imperfections
common to and inherent in its nature. It rouses
our repugnance without exciting our fear or our
attention; and we here, doubtless, behold the
obscure motive of the phenomenon of which I
have been speaking.

I shall finish this letter by making you observe,
en passant, that the action of fear is likewise a

motive one, whilst the evil which we fear depends on the will of a free agent ; and that, in
this case, the motives differ much according to
difference of character and circumstances : for
sometimes we strive to move by prayer and submission, and sometimes to alarm by a display of
firmness and courage.   Pride and flattery are
employed according to circumstances and dispositions of persons.

LETTER XV.

The Desire of removing or destroying an Evil—Different from Choler—Anger sometimes vented on inanimate Objects —The well known Story of Xerxes—A Reflection thereon —Dreadful Effects of Passion—Remark of a great Man of Antiquity—Plutarch—Opinion of Seneca—Cursory Hint to Dramatic Artists.

THE desire to remove or destroy an evil may be a very different thing from choler ; notwithstanding it is only under the traits of this passion [*which*, for as much as I know, confounds itself with the desire of punishment and vengeance, according to the opinion of all the ancient philosophers] that it has its most marked and characteristical operations.

The soul, agitated by this desire, manifests no other sign in the body save ardour and resolution ; to which, perhaps, the expression of the other affections associates itself; such, for example, as those of fear, terror, and displeasure. But while sensible and reasonable beings purposely cause us to experience pain and chagrin,

because they have been disgusted with us under some point of view, considering us in the
light of individuals not dangerous, or of persons
they may offend with impunity, without having
any thing to fear from us in return; as when
they wound us in the dark, without fear of a
discovery. When we find out all this, when we
remark that our enemy feels a malignant satisfaction at the grief his address has implanted in
our wounded sensibilities, the desire of vengeance
inflames the heart, and we feel ourselves spurred
on to *return* the woes we have endured on those
who have been the authors of our sufferings.
Thus the roaring torrent breaks down the opposing barrier, and tears down every object which
impedes it with resistless violence: at the terrible aspect of these destructive effects, the cruel
joy of our enemy is converted into alarm and
grief; whilst our own bitter chagrin is trans-
formed into the delicious sentiment arising from
the idea of our own proper puissance, and the
terror which it scatters abroad. The result of
this corresponds with what the moral philosophers have long since observed, *i. e.* that this resentment naturally rouses itself against free and
thinking agents; that it is less natural when exerted against animals, which, not being able either

to offend or to irritate us, have only the faculty
of hurting us; and that it is quite unnatural,
when exerted against objects passive or inanimate.

The extravagant idea of Xerxes, when he
threatened to chain and lash the sea, has been
treated as a species of delirium.   It is probable,
however, that a despot, less accustomed than
other men to the mortifying idea of his impo-
tence and his dependency, might have found a
species of consolation in blinding himself to such
a point as to conceive that he might avenge his
own torments on the vexed sea, and that he was
formidable enough to make the ocean feel his
vengeance.   Thus, as I have been saying, *choler*
adds energy to all the exterior parts of the body,
but chiefly arms those most proper to seize,
attack, or destroy; swelled by the blood and
humours which are thither carried in abundance,
they agitate themselves with a convulsive violence.   The inflamed eyes roll in their orbits,
and dart forth fiery glances; the hands and teeth
manifest a kind of interior tumult, by the grind-
ing of one and the agitation of the others.   It
is the same kind of eagerness which the mad
bull and furious bear display, to make use of the
arms with which Nature has furnished them:

moreover, the veins are swelled, especially those about the neck and temples; all the visage is inflamed, on account of the superabundance of blood carried up to it: but this redness resembles not that occasioned by desire or love; the movements are more hurried and more violent; the step is heavy, irregular, impetuous.—You will object to me, that these changes do not always take place—that the visage as often turns pale as red. I answer, that the desire of vengeance may change itself into the disagreeable sentiment of the offence received, and then *vice versa :* or, if you prefer giving the name of choler to this reunited sentiment, I shall say then, " This choler is composed of the chagrin of the offence received, and of the desire of taking vengeance for it."

In reuniting all the gestures and actions of a man in choler, the picture will be a disgusting one; particularly if you add the poisoned foam which sometimes drops from the lower lip :—at this sight the tranquil observer will conceive the greatest horror at a passion which can ravage the noble countenance of man with such infernal violence. I remember Plutarch makes one of his great men say, " That he should be thankful to any servant who would place a lookingglass before his eyes, at each approach of anger; because that, seeing himself in such an unnatural condition, he should certainly learn to detest the passion." But, in my opinion, the servant would show himself more wise in leaving the mirror alone, as he would run a great chance of having it thrown at his head. It was otherwise with Minerva, of whom Plutarch recounts, that she threw away her flute, because she perceived the grimaces (in a river) which she made while playing on that instrument.

The mind of Minerva was calm; and, being a woman, it was for her interest to look beautiful, and not to disfigure her face by distortions. She played on a flute to please: but the man in choler wishes to inspire terror.—Let us hear what Seneca says:

"Speculo equidem neminem deterritum ab ira credo. Qui ad speculum venerat, ut se mutaret, jam mutaverat. Iratis quidem nulla est formosior effigies, quam atrox et horrida, qualesque esse, etiam videri volunt."—*De Ira.* l. ii. c. 35.

I am wandering from my subject without perceiving it: but what can I say, after this author, of the gestures of the desire of vengeance? He

has given a description in each of the three books
he has written on choler, and has there developed
the most slight shades of this passion with so
much eloquence that his most warm admirer
could not avoid exclaiming, " Ubique diffuse et
cur toties?"—Choose those passages which appear to you the most just or beautiful : I shall
content myself with offering a slight remark for
the consideration of the actor ; to wit—that, in
the imitation of choler, he ought to propose another end to himself than the natural imitation
of a passion whose effects so easily become disgusting: he must guard in this, more than in
any other passion, against overcharging what is
in itself so hideous and unpleasant to the eye
and to the imagination.

LETTER XVI.

Of Vengeance and Choler—Their Effects—Anger and Vengeance often mistake their Objects—An Instance in Othello —In Anthony and Cleopatra—Dreadful Effects of Rage — Operating to Self Molestation—The Passion of Love acting in a manner somewhat similar towards surrounding Objects—An Example from Mr. Cumberland's Comedy of the West Indian.

THERE is a something of malice in the question you put to me; I mean in that particular one where you ask in what class of expression I should choose to range *choler* or desire of vengeance.   I suppose you slily mean to make me sensible of all that is vague and ambiguous in my classifications.   These classifications are, in your opinion, more adapted to create confusion than to prevent it.   But recollect, I have no where pretended to tell you that my mode has appeared unobjectionable even to myself, or that it is by any means conformable to the precise and rigid rules of logic.

You say that, according to my argument, all changes of the blood ought to be referred to phisiological causes; but that we, nevertheless, in sudden colouring and paleness, find something analogous to the situation of the soul. The spirits are carried with energy towards the extremities of the body when a man is thinking of an enemy, when occupied in rumination on his personal prowess, or when the mental faculties are flattered with the ideas of approaching vengeance.

Your remark that anger frequently quits its real object, and fixes on others totally foreign and extraneous, is extremely just, and I feel much indebted to you for it.

Notwithstanding this, I cannot avoid expressing my surprise that, out of so many examples quoted by Hume, from whom you confess to have borrowed the foregoing observation, you should have selected the precise one which appears to me the least forcible of them all. Iago has roused the jealousy of Othello, in the tragedy of that name, by equivocal signs, and circumstances calculated to excite his suspicions, which do not, however, seem sufficiently founded to make their effects be resented on Desdemona, their natural object. The disorder and anxiety awakened in his soul by these suggestions, excite his momentary rage, even against Iago himself, who as yet appears not only innocent, but friendly in his eyes.

Othello.   Villain, be sure you prove my love a whore ;
Be sure of it ; give me the ocular proof ;

[Catching hold of him.

Or, by the worth of mine eternal soul,
Thou hadst been better have been born a dog,
Than answer my wak'd wrath.

    Iago.   Is it come to this ?

    Othello.   If thou dost slander her, and torture me,
Never pray more : abandon all remorse ;
On horror's head horrors accumulate :
Do deeds to make Heaven weep, all earth amaz'd,
For nothing canst thou to damnation add,
Greater than that.

    Iago.   O Grace ! O Heaven, defend me !
Are you a man ? have you a soul, or sense ?
God be wi' you ; take mine office.—Oh, wretched fool
That liv'st to make thine honesty a vice !

See the fine Scene, Othello, Act iii.

You will pardon me for differing with you, and
saying that, in my *my* opinion, the choler is here
directed to its right object ; for Othello, attached
heart and soul to his Desdemona, and horrified
with the cruel and insurportable torments of jealousy, visibly abandons the suspicions he had entertained against the virtue of his wife, and clearly
delivers himself up to those of an opposite nature,
to wit, his suspicions of the integrity and vera-
city of Iago.   And hence arises a remark, confirmed by experience, to wit, that the bearer of
ill news becomes hateful on his own account : I
shall illustrate this observation by a very striking

example, which occurs in Shakspeare's play of
Antony and Cleopatra:

Anthony.   Moon and stars !
Whip him:—Were 't twenty of the greatest tributaries
That do acknowledge Cæsar, should I find them
So saucy with the hand of she here, (What's her name,
Since she was Cleopatra?)—Whip him, fellows,
Till, like a boy, you see him cringe his face,
And whine aloud for mercy: Take him hence.
    Messenger.   Mark Anthony,—
    Anthony.   Tug him away: being whipped,
Bring him again:—This Jack of Cæsar's
Shall bear us an errand to him.—
                    [*Exeunt Messenger and Attendants.*
    Cleopatra.   Wherefore is this?
    Anthony.   To let a fellow that will take rewards,
And say, God quit you, be familiar with
My playfellow, your hand; this kingly seal,
And plighter of high hearts!—O! that I were
Upon the hill of Basan, to outroar
The horned herd! for I have savage cause;
And to proclaim it civilly, were like
A halter'd neck, which does the hangman thank
For being yare about him —Is he whipp'd?

                    (*Re-enter Messenger and Attendant.*)

    Attendant.   Soundly, my Lord.
    Anthony.   Cried he? and asked he mercy?
    Attendant.   He did ask favour.
    Anthony.   If that thy father live, let him repent
Thou wast not made his daughter; and be thou sorry
To follow Cæsar in his triumph, since
Thou hast been whipp'd for following him: henceforth,
The white hand of a lady fever thee,
Shake thou to look on't.—Get thee back to Cæsar,

Tell him thy entertainment: Look, thou say,
He makes me angry with him: for he seems
Proud and disdainful; harping on what I *am;*
Not what he knew I *was:* He makes me angry;
And at this time most easy 'tis to do't;
When my good stars, that were my former guides,
Have empty left their orbs, and shot their fires
Into the abism of hell.   If he mislike
My speech, and what is done; tell him, he has
Hipparchus, my enfranchised bondman, whom
He may at pleasure whip, or hang, or torture,
As he shall like, to quit me: Urge it thou:
Hence, with thy stripes!   Begone!

Cæsar had raised the jealousy of Anthony, and
not being able to punish the wrong in his person, he avenges it on the Messenger.

Notwithstanding this example, if we adopt the
explication of Aristotle, the anger here personified may not be entirely directed to an object of
indifference, or on false grounds; for the tranquillity and icy phlegm of the Messenger, a witness of the bitter agony suffered, might appear
to him a piece of contempt, and an offence which
might naturally excite his bile.   Besides, we are
sure that it would not have been the innocent
Messenger, but the perjured lover who would
have felt the force of his resentment, had *power*
seconded the *inclination.*   The effects of revenge

will also be sometimes wreaked even on inanimate objects. Do we not often see persons rub letters in their hands, stamp them under their feet, or tear them with their teeth? Perchance we shall be able to throw some light on the subject, by making an abstraction of those objects which are innocent and foreign, by generalizing our observations, and establishing it as a truth, that the desire of vengeance is a furious passion, of which the boiling symptoms are not easily allayed in the human heart—and that, while it cannot exercise its fury on the desired object, it seizes on such *inanimate* ones as are at all related to it; and when none of this kind can be found, will fly .to objects different and innocent, and wreak its fury by trampling, beating, tearing, and defacing them—and when it cannot be satisfied in this manner, it resembles canine hunger, and hurries the individual even to violence upon himself. This terrible desire once excited in the heart of man, all his nervous system is in the greatest disorder, and he is disturbed by a continual disquietude:—rather than remain idle, and not wreak its rage on *something*, it will bite the lip till the blood flows, gnaw the nails, and rend the hair, without knowing any bounds to its fury:—like the Italian who, after having lost his whole fortune at the gaming table, tore out his inside with his concealed hand, whilst an apparent tranquillity kept place in all the traits of his countenance. The hands, the feet, the teeth will instinctively seek for employment.

To smite suddenly on the left hand with the right is a declaration of some mistake, anger, or indignation. Seneca attributes this to anger; for, in his description of an angry man, he writes thus: " Parum explanatis vocibus, sermo præruptus, et complosa sæpius manus." Bulwer observes that Petronius presents us with this gesture of anger and grief, " infractes manibus ingemuit."

In the anger or ill humour which is yet concentrated we remark their unquiet agitation. The man in this situation bites the lower lip gently—he agitates the foot, or stamps on the earth with it. He arranges and readjusts his clothes, he rubs his hat, or, with his hand behind his ear, fumbles among the hairs of his head. The circumstance of the hand being involuntarily conveyed to the hair proves that a disagreeable alteration has taken place in the skin which covers the skull, and has there produced uncomfortable sensations—an effect equally caused by fear and terror. This deviation 'of the affection

of which we have been speaking, from the principal object to those with which it is connected,
or to others absolutely foreign, may *perhaps* be
an essential point, which holds good, more or
less, in all our desires.   We know that it takes
place in *that fever* which, arrived at its greatest
height, carries the idea of danger to objects
the most innocent; and, trembling at the slightest noise, starts from the breeze that whispers
through the foliage.   Here call to your mind
the sublime picture of *Æneas* carrying the aged
Anchises upon his shoulders, and leading the
young *Ascanius* by the hand :

> Ferimur per opaca locorum.
> Et me, quem dudum non ulla injecta movebant
> Tela, neque adverso glomerati ex agmine Graii,
> Nunc omnes terrent auræ : sonus excitat omnis
> Suspensum, et pariter comitique onerique timentem.

Among the variety of motions peculiar to the
hand Mr. M. W. Sharpe, in his *Essay on Gesture*,
has observed, that to beckon with the raised
hands is accounted by all nations a sign of crav-
ing audience and entreating a favourable silence.
How considerable an expression this gesture was
ever accounted may be collected out of the
Office of the Common Crier, whom we find

among the ancients commanded silence by the hand alone; which gesture, if it were used by the Criers of our Courts of Justice, it is thought would be more proper and significant to procure silence than by making more noise to restore peace, confounding one auricular disturbance with another. When Commodus the Emperor was set on his throne to behold those famous actors who were to celebrate a sacred agon, or pageant, in honour of Jupiter Capitolinus, and the theatre full of spectators; before the performance commenced suddenly one started on the stage in a philosopher's habit, with a staff in his hand and scrip on his shoulder, half naked, stood still, and, beckoning *with his hand* for silence, discovered the treason of Perennius to Commodus.

To lift up the right hand to heaven is the form and ceremony of an oath; an expression first used by the Patriarchs. To extend and raise both hands to heaven implies a double oath. Lauretus says, the lifting up the right and left hand signifies an oath with a commination and a promise. In the King's Collection of pictures is a very fine one, of which the subject is Hannibal swearing eternal enmity to Rome; and to render the oath of greater import, an old man holds up a boy's left hand that he might denounce a double oath. Marius, in the battle of the Cymbres, in promising a hundred oxen lifted up the hand to heaven.

To hold up the hand is a token of approbation and giving suffrage. This practice, which was in use among the ancients, has continued to this day. Our members of parliament are first nominated by a show of hands; and this practice has even descended to clubs and societies of the lower orders of people.

To wave the hand from us, the palm outward, is the gesture of repulsion and dismissal. Nothing can be more common than to shake our hand to those departing either by sea or land, as a last adieu. This gesture is equally strong where we wish to forbid or keep off: for instance, suppose a person attending on an expiring friend just as he is about to breathe his last gasp, a busy, officious nurse at this moment enters the room; the attendant, *still keeping his eyes* fixed upon the dying patient, motions with his hand for the nurse to be gone; she departs, for the language of the hand in this instance is *too* expressive not to be understood : on the contrary, should the hand beckon, the palm turned inward, the nurse and relatives would pour round the bed

in the most joyful expectation of the patient's
approaching recovery : this motion of the hand
draws to you, as it were, the object of your attention, and is a gesture apparent to any one of
observation.

To shake the fist at any one signifies anger
and defiance. The Italian vulgar constantly re-
sent the indignity of this minatory agitation of
the hand exhibited against them ; and it is the
sure prelude to a battle amongst the lower order
of English.

To extend the hand hollow is the characteristic gesture of begging. There is a certain form
or semblance of the thing implied in this unusual
capacity of the hand ; from the natural signification of this gesture that severe adage of Erasmus
had its origin, which taxed the lucrative greedi-
ness of the Athenians : " Atheniensis vel moriens,
cavat manum." Marcus Antonius the imperial
philosopher, when he came to Rome, in an oration to the people said, he had been absent many
years : the multitude cried out eight years ; and,
with stretched out hands hollowed in this dish-
like form, craved that they might receive so
many aurei, at which the Emperor smiled, and
said " Let it be eight ;" and afterwards gave
them eight aurei, a piece which is two hundred

drachms. To hold out the hand is a mean way
of begging, from which it is conceived the reason
why most painters have chosen to represent Belisarius with his helmet stretched out. Vandyke
however, in his celebrated picture on this subject,
has stretched out the hand of Belisarius; and
perhaps from this cause the expression of those
about him are much finer than the figure of Belisarius himself.

In the rhetorical actions of the hand, as in all
others, the happy medium ought to be observed;
for the action of the hand should be full of dignity and magnanimous resolution, making it a
liberal and full index of the mind. Hamlet's
advice to the players should be read by the orator and painter as well as by the tragedian ; and
every public speech and picture should consist
of a certain moderation of gesture ; no incom-
posed rashness, or a too daring garb of action ;
neither superfinical demeanor, nor, on the other
side, a bashful fearfulness which is sure to discou-
rage and disappoint the purpose of necessary
motion : yet of the two extremes it is better
that modesty should prevail over impertinence of
gesture ; the tempering of gesture is not only to
be observed from the things themselves, but also
from the age and condition of the orator : a

smooth and calm action becomes an aged man endued with authority, which to one in the flower of youth would be considered sluggish negligence. An orator should first consider with whom, and in whose presence he is about to speak; if in the House of Commons, Courts of Law, or in the hearing of a prince, another action is required from that of speaking to an assembly of people, or party of gay young men. Concerning this happy medium there is a national decorum, imposed by *time* and *place;* for, according to the manners of that climate in which we converse, moderation may admit of various constructions. In Italy a superabundant gesture is esteemed, and is necessary; in France, he is not à la mode and a complete Monsieur who is not expert in the discoursing garb of the hand; in Germany, and with us in England, for in our national complexion we are nearly allied, moderation in gesture and gravity is esteemed the greater virtue. The Spaniards have another standard of moderation and gravity, according to the lofty genius of Spain, where the hands are as often principals as accessaries to their proud expressions. As our language is grown rich by the adoption of words of all nations, and so altered from the old Teutonic, if the rule of moderation

be persevered in we may with decorum and gravity meet the hand of any of the warmer nations
half way, with the manual adjuncts of our expressions.

Compound Gestures principally consist of one
or both hands applied to the head : also the various direction the fingers take, making up an
extensive catalogue of expressive signification.
It is a remark worthy of notice that the ancients
were famous for their calculations entirely done
by the fingers. Hortensius the orator usually
set his arguments all on a row at his fingers
ends. In the Areopagite Schools, or Council-
house at Athens, they painted Chrysippus with
his fingers in this posture for the signification of
numbers. Modern artists when they would exhibit arithmetic in their pictures observe the
same gesture. If this manual arithmetic were
fully known, it would bring to light many difficult and obscure passages of old writers, which
cannot be understood without it : their manner
was to reckon upon the left hand until they came
to one hundred, and from thence to the right
hand. These postures were recorded among the
Egyptian letters, or hieroglyphics, as unfit to be
prostituted by the vulgar. Many of these nu-
merical postures of the fingers are found in the

ancient statues: the Statue of Janus, in the Capitol, exhibited in the hands the number three hundred and sixty-five, thereby intimating the days of the year, and that he is the god of times and ages.

It is remarked by Mr. Henry Siddons, that the desire which carries us towards an object offers also something similar in certain circumstances: I shall find future occasion to speak of this. I shall here confine myself to observe, in a few words, that satisfied and happy love diffuses itself in caresses and in acts of beneficence, even towards those objects which are *strange* and *foreign*, not only in the absence of the beloved object, but even in the midst of possession. The fiery West Indian, in Mr. Cumberland's charming comedy, embraces the whole company, after obtaining the hand of his dear Charlotte.

When I quote from the works of Mr. Cumberland, I ever imagine that I quote from Nature herself—since it is from the inexhaustible mine of that goddess whence all his characters are drawn: his dramatis personæ invariably act as persons in real life would behave under the impressions of similar circumstances. No one has written more naturally ; and yet there is scarcely any dramatic writer so classically correct : his

fund of humour is deep and various; his characters have every faculty of exciting risibility, and
yet remain independent of the witticisms, manners, dress, or politics of the day. We trace
nothing of the caricature in his compositions,
nor do his clowns and footmen ever branch forth
into the sentimental luxuriancy of sages and
philosophers, to draw down a few plaudits from
the auditors: his gentlemen, on the other hand,
never act like valets or madmen, to excite the
ridiculous by the total violation of the possible
or the probable. Major O' Flaherty is a gentleman in manners and in sentiments: of this
characteristical dignity he never once loses view
during five delightful acts; yet the stage cannot
produce a more delightful or a more entertaining
specimen of Hibernian whimsicality.

We have now a performer on the boards of
one of our theatres who defies all competition in
characters of humorous Irishmen: in the whole
range of these characters, which he delineates so
exquisitely well, there is not one where he stands
more conspicuous than in Mr. Cumberland's humorous, generous, open-hearted soldier. I could
mention many other elucidations of the happy
genius of our English Terence—but

To gild refined gold—to paint the lily—
To throw a perfume on the violet—
Is wasteful and ridiculous excess.

King John.

Mr. Cumberland is a first-rate scholar, and has made use of this advantage in all his dramatic writings : he has fully felt the force of the following Horatian maxim :

Si quid inexpertum Scenæ committis, et audes
Personam formare novam ; servetur ad imum
Qualis ab incepto processerit, et sibi constet.
Difficile est propriè communia dicere.

My praise can be no compliment to

" The observed of all *observers ;*"

yet shall I boldly lay my little leaf of myrtle at his feet : for as it has been remarked, that the bravest men are commonly the most merciful, so is it likewise my creed, that the most learned men are the most indulgent ; and in the full spirit of this sentiment I make my bow to the author of the elegant West Indian, and to the bold delineator of the manly, the affecting, the sublime Penruddock.

LETTER XVII.

The Judgment of a Philosopher—On Envy and Hatred—Similarity of general Appearances—Difficulty of presenting them in one Point of View—Examples—From Cato—Cæsar—Othello—The Gradations of Jealousy in Love.

IF an author attaches himself principally to the *exterior* signs or phenomena of the passions, it would be unreasonable to expect from him a too rigid adherence to his classifications, or to look for the same minute explications which are given by the natural philosopher who has passed whole years in the study of their *internal* effects; for so difficultly various is the perplexing research that where one man thinks he contemplates a unity of appearance another imagines that he can discern a hundred ramifications and diversities: for as many rivers may be derived from a single source so likewise may a single river be the result of a variety of springs. As this is an object of some importance, and not easily to be explained by general reflections and observations, I find it necessary to call in the support of a few examples. A philosopher may be able to discriminate the feeling of *envy* from that kind of displeasure some men experience at the contemplation of the more successful fortunes of others: they refer the origin of the one to that *self-love* which is common to the nature of man, whilst they attribute the other to a species of *personal dislike*. It might be said that Cato, seeing the enemies of the republic exalted to the most lucrative and dignified situations in Rome, experienced this sentiment, because the persons so upraised by fortune were his determined opponents; whilst Cæsar and Pompey were bona fide envious of the successes of each other. Now this distinction is as true as it appears remarkable. To appreciate it justly, however, it will be requisite to peer into the most secret recesses of the soul, as it is by this attentive observance alone that we shall be able to account for the outward operation of the gestures.

Both the affections we have been describing spread an outward visible air of chagrin over the countenance; they give a kind of suspicious glance to the eye, and avert the body, with a sort of involuntary emotion, from the

object which gives birth to their suspicion or
their jealousy.   We may, perhaps, expect to
find two descriptions correspondent to each of
these sentiments.   Yet the perplexed philosopher, when he has to speak of hatred, finds himself compelled to revert to what he has before
said on the subject of jealousy; half owning that
he has failed in his attempts at attaining any
characteristical signs which can distinguish the
one from the other.   Yet, if there is really a
perfect resemblance between the traits of hatred
and those of jealousy, why should any artist involve *himself* in an unnecessary trouble?—why
does he not spare his reader the fatigue of poring
over his words or his drawings ?   But the truth
is, that what takes place with jealousy and hatred
may be referred to what is said on the subject of
envy and malevolence.

Is jealousy really only to be recognised under the guise of hatred ?—when she ceases to
assume this garb is she at all altered in essentials ?

I am much deceived, or you now begin to
perceive a kind of unity in the *source* of these
different affections of the soul. If you select
the jealousy of ambition for the object of your

contemplation, you will find a variety of ramifications: you will sometimes view it connected
with *shame*—at others it will appertain to a displeasure closely bordering upon anger. In such
a complex mixture of sentiments and feelings
how difficult must be the task of giving such
marked traits which shall not interfere with a
correct delineation of the passion! How shall
we distinguish the tears shed by young Cæsar,
during the perusal of the life of Alexander, from
any other kind of noble grief?

Though we may be able to denote the general traits of hatred, grief, despair, ironical laughter, with all the other expressions, mixed or simple, which appertain to *jealousy*, yet it will be
difficult to reunite and bring them together, so
as to occasion such a delineation as cannot be
confounded with similar affections.

Le Brun has marked the expressions of hatred;
but, as hatred is not always the companion of
jealousy, he has not cleared the difficulties I have
mentioned.

Had this artist been compelled to represent
the passion, in a picture, under the semblance of
an allegorical being, he would only have seized
one point of view, and would therefore have displayed his judgment in the selection of *that one*

which offered the most self-evident and *general expression.*

Rapture and despair are the words which serve to denote the highest climax of our agreeable or painful sensations.   But rapture sometimes consists as much in the delicate languors of pleasure as in the more animated expressions of boisterous felicity.

Despair may be delineated by the most humble dejection of the soul, and also by its more furious and ungoverned transports.—What unity can an author indicate here!—Should he paint rapture as a soft sensation of voluptuous indolence, with eyes swimming in pleasure, and half concealed under their lids; I might ask him, in my turn, whether a physiognomy, lively, gay, and sparkling with the most vivid joy; eyes floating in splendour, arms stretched out, the body bounding from earth, and dancing in the wanton air;—I would ask him, I repeat, whether he would not recognise the required sentiment under this delineation also?   *(See Plates* XXV. *and* XXVI.)   To regain the unity, it must be necessary to take the word rapture in a more strict and literal sense, and to explain it by that spiritual and voluptuous intuition which forms the charm of a romantic imagination.

This resource will avail nothing, however, when we come to examine despair : for if we contemplate the famous print of Count Ugolino, exhausted by famine, and already bearing a strong resemblance to a dead corpse, we shall there find those traits of despair which are indicated by the idea of *suicide*.

To appear with fainting and dejected hands is a posture of fear, abasement of mind, an abject and vanquished courage, and utter despair. Thus Polybius wishing to denote the pusillanimity of Prusias, king of Bythynia, in his demeanour to the Roman senate, says, " Demissis manibus lumen salutavit." This gesture of utter despair is frequently portrayed in the hands of the Virgin Mary, at the foot of the cross.

Leonardo da Vinci says, " *You may represent a man abandoned to despair, holding a knife in his hand, with which he strikes himself; after having torn open his garments with one hand, he enlarges his wound : he will be upright, with the feet straggling the one from the other, or with his body bent, as if in the action of falling to the ground.*"

You will please to remark that the above sketch is only a project of this inestimable artist ; and that he is here speaking of what *may* and not of what *ought* to be done. This is despair *personified*—such as it ought to be when represented in a painting. As I spoke of *jealousy* in the beginning of my letter, I wish to mention one species of that affection which had escaped me in the difficulty of arranging my notions. I allude to the jealousy of love. If you examine this species of suspicion, the poetical *Proteus* will no longer be regarded as a fictitious being :—jealousy, like this god, every moment assumes a new form ; anxiety, tears, impatience, the smile of derision, the searching glance of doubt, the bitter complaint, the broken hearted despondency, violence, fury, *murder !* Behold the gradation of sentiments succeeding to each other in the bosom of *Othello*.

LETTER XXVIII.

*Descartes and Le Brun—The Source of agreeable and dis-
agreeable Affections—Examination of the agreeable Sentiment—Of Joy and Tranquillity—Their physical Effects
—The Joy of the proud Man—Of the Lover—Fine Passage of Xenophon—The vain Man—Of Courage and
Firmness—Animated Description—A beautiful Speech
quoted from Shakspeare's Tragedy of Cymbeline.*

DESCARTES makes an express distinction between
corporeal sensation and the passions of the soul.
Le Brun, although a faithful follower of the
philosopher in other instances, abandons him in
this : if this desertion is not couched in express
words, it is at least tacitly allowed by the artist
when speaking of physical grief. I shall not
adopt the opinions of either of these celebrated
men ; fearful lest I should be induced to pass
over the rules relating to corporeal expression in
too cursory a manner, or that I may find myself
compelled to enter into details too tedious for
your perusal ; and, after all, these rules would
be of no very important consequence to the actor,
whose instruction is the principal object of these

researches. Notwithstanding these considerations, we must not absolutely neglect the scrutiny of physical effects ; for, as they are not unfrequently consequences of the interior movements of the soul, their expression will carry us back to the original source. Whilst Othello, staggering from one side to the other, lifts one hand to his head, as if conscious of his approaching fit, and strikes the other upon his convulsed and agonized heart—whilst his tongue can only utter broken, half-connected sentences ; we recognise in these external sensations of the *body* the modifications which affect the *soul.*

I have previously stated that the affections generate from our sense of our own failings or perfections—the first giving rise to the agreeable, and the second to the unpleasing affections : now their reunion is the cause of the *mixed affections.* A similar sentiment has frequently but not always a mixed expression : consequently a considerable number of this kind may be ranged in the class of simple sentiments.

According to several philosophers, neither pure grief nor pure pleasure occasions the shedding of tears : to make them flow it is necessary that the agreeable should mingle with the disagreeable, or *per contra.*

Let us commence, then, with an examination of the more pleasing affections, and leave the disagreeable ones for an ulterior disquisition. It is natural to select what most flatters the imagination : in a basket of fruits, who will not give the preference to the most beautiful and the best flavoured ? There are some men so happily tempered that the most perfect equilibrium of the humours permits the blood to flow without obstruction or impediment in the delicate vessels —and the natural consequence of this is freedom in the progression of their ideas, a mirth and vivacity cheering the heart, and beaming on the visage ; and pictures of smiling felicity are for ever present to the contemplation of these favoured children of mortality : when happy events operate on their exterior, we do not simply observe a serenity and satisfaction but that superior degree of agreeable sentiment to which I shall give the exclusive name of joy. In the play which this joy produces we remark the most perfect analogy, the most exact impressions of a soul which opens (as we may say) every avenue to flattering ideas, in measuring the movements of the body exactly upon the degree of velocity, of pliableness, and facility which reign in the progression of his clear and governing conceptions.

The countenance is open and frank in all parts, the front is serene, the head elevated with grace between the shoulders, the eloquent eye presents its full globe shining with splendour, the mouth presents that amiable " Semihians labellum," as as Catullus calls it ; the arms and hands are detached from the body ; the walk is sprightly and gay ; lightness, activity, and grace reign in the movements of all the limbs.

You must conclude from hence that the phenomena of joy offer themselves under amiable traits, and that they are replete with elegance and beauty ; and you may draw this inference from it, viz. that they will be so much the more characteristical, and their resemblance with this affection will be so much the more marking as the ideas which occupy the soul are more gracious or beautiful, and as these ideas more or less favour the analogies indicated. The joy of the proud man who beholds the completion of his ambitious projects will make his whole face expand, and will confer activity and lightness on the movements of his body. But whilst ideas grand, elevated, and vast actually occupy his soul, we shall find there is more or less to do away of this sentiment ; we shall here be apt to remark less of pure joy than of a *mixture* of *joy* and *pride*.

The lover, whose whole soul wanders over soft, beautiful, and voluptuous ideas, on the contrary, will show his joy under the characteristics of a frank happiness, *pure* and complete. It is useless to observe that this sentiment has its degrees, as well as the sentiment itself. The highest point of rapture or transport will be a reinforcement to those traits I have just been indicating. In truth, those traits entirely seem to lose all their grace from the moment the joy begins to grow too giddy or too boisterous, or when it degenerates into a petulance which throws the face into grimaces, and transforms the soft and easy movements of the body into the boundings and caperings of a mountebank. The actions to which joy commonly delivers itself are those which produce the most lively impressions upon all the senses; such, for example, as good cheer, smiling, singing, clapping of hands, dancing, and a desire to communicate with those whom we wish to interest in the felicity of our lot; a species of corruption (if I dare thus express myself) which operates by embraces, presents, protestations of amity, benefits, and above all by caresses lavished on those from whom we expect the most lively and most intimate sympathy, on account of their attachment, the conformity of their station, or their full participation of the common happiness.

Men who have run the same dangers and endured the same misfortunes embrace each other in the first transport, mingling tears of joy with their reciprocal felicitations. Xenophon has a fine passage of this kind. You know that the ten thousand Greeks had to struggle against innumerable obstacles and dangers in their famous retreat *.

When they came to the summit of the mountain, the sea suddenly burst on their sight : the joy was general—the soldiers could not refrain from tears, but embraced their generals and captains.

Suppress for the present the novelty and celerity of the impression caused by happy and particular events : let the perfection with which the soul is occupied be of a permanent quality, and give leisure and repose to intuition itself; then the sentiment will in truth preserve much of softness and contentment, but the characteristic of *joy* will vanish, and all will depend on the nature of the idea which ought to be expressed by the gesture. You will presently have the proof in

---

* Επει δε αφικοντο παντες επι το ακρον εν ταυθα δη περιεβαλλον αλληλυς και Στρατεγυς, και λοχαγυς δακρυοντες.

that personal satisfaction which agreeably affects the man while he considers perfection as a part or inherent quality in *himself.*

Does any one admire the charms and beauty of his *own* figure, or the activity and the grace of his movements; then the soft smile of internal contentment, the vivacity of soul, the gaiety of gesture remain; he leaps, runs, sings,—a thousand attitudes succeed, that he may be able to look at and admire himself under several points of view.

If the prudence and address with which we have gained a point excite our self-admiration, then a fugitive smile will just simper on the cheek, and play about the lips; the eye will contract itself, the look will become more lively, the steps more slow and oblique; the index sign will, perhaps, be showing the person gulled; and, in order to guide the intention of the interlocutor as mysteriously as the intrigue has been conducted, we shall jog him with the end of the elbow put out of sight. *(See Plate* XXVII.)

If dignity, force of mind, power, or any other superior merit be the matter in debate, the man measures by his corporeal height his own qualities with those who are deprived of similar advantages; he erects his head with dignity, assuming a serious and pensive air, and his whole deportment becomes more cold and more concentrated, as the idea of his self-merit gives him the greater degree of satisfaction.

The plenitude of his ideas occasions the enlargement of his steps and his movements; the tardiness of the developement of these ideas, the natural consequence of this plenitude, renders his step long, pompous, and majestic.

If birth, rank, fortune, or any of these foreign and insignificant advantages, which cannot give a man any real sentiment of his proper merit, and whose enjoyment depends on the effects produced in the minds of others, occupy the mind, then the concentrated and tranquil air which belongs to genuine pride degenerates into conceit and vanity. Little satisfied with silent pomp, he struts along, resting the body on the wide-stretched legs, the arms and hands are spread abroad, the head and whole body thrown back *(as in Plate* XXVIII).

Does the matter relate to courage, firmness, or power of resistance, immediately the corporeal energies rouse, the body becomes more compact, the muscles are stretched, the neck stiffens, the knees contract, and the head sinks itself between the elevated shoulders *(as exemplified in Plate* XXIX).

I cannot tell how far figures may express my meaning; your observing sagacity must supply the deficiency.

After what I have said above, concerning the admiration which grand and elevated corporeal objects inspire, you doubtless have already remarked that, at all times, when plunged in the contemplation of an object, we do not separate by abstraction our proper selves from the idea which we entertain of this object; we seek to adopt its qualities, and to render ourselves semblable to it. We aggrandize ourselves with that which is great; we elevate ourselves with the sublime; we soften ourselves with what is tender.

In the intuition of the moral affections this forgetfulness, or rather this advantageous exchange of *self* with another, is much more easy than while it operates with regard to physical objects; and this exchange is precisely the first source of that intellectual voluptuousness which the delineation of elevated, firm, and noble characters, and the recital of grand and intrepid actions inspired by the love of humanity make us experience. We rouse in ourselves the pride,

the dignity, the warmth of soul, or the soft sensibility which we suppose in our heroes; and, in
this manner, all these sentiments, in becoming
sufficiently strong to produce visible modifications, ought to depict themselves in our gestures
and in our mien.   You have an example in the
young Polydore of Shakspeare, whilst listening to
the recital of old Morgan.

The supposed father of this young prince thus
describes his emotion:

How hard it is, to hide the sparks of nature !
These boys know little, they are sons to the king;
Nor Cymbeline dreams that they are alive.
They think, they are mine: and, though train'd up thus
        meanly
I' the cave, wherein they bow, their thoughts do hit
The roofs of palaces; and nature prompts them,
In simple and low things, to prince it, much
Beyond the trick of others.   This Polydore,—
The heir of Cymbeline and Britain, whom
The king his father called Guiderius,—Jove !
When on my three-foot stool I sit, and tell
The warlike feats I have done, his spirits fly out
Into my story: say,—*Thus mine enemy fell ;*
And thus I set my foot on his neck ; even then
The princely blood flows in his cheek, he sweats,
Strains his young nerves, and puts himself in posture
That acts my words.   The younger brother, Cadwal,
(Once Arvirágus,) in as like a figure,
Strikes life into my speech, and shows much
More his own conceiving.

                    Cymbeline, Act iii.

Thus, every time we enter into the feelings and the thoughts of another, there is nothing new concerning the sentiments which we transplant (if I may so express myself) from his soul into our own.   But when we abstract ourselves, or when, perhaps, we place ourselves in opposition to that which occupies us, two sentiments then offer themselves at once, to wit, love and veneration ; sentiments of which the proper expressions are very remarkable.

LETTER XIX.

The Expression of Veneration—Of Love—A Remark on the Modifications which these Affections borrow from their Object.

VENERATION is the admiration of a moral being, to such a point as to own our own inferiority in a comparison : it is only by this comparison that veneration becomes an affection of the heart, which, as such, does not consequently belong to the class of agreeable affections.

Notwithstanding there is always something satisfactory in the aggregate of this sentiment, namely, while the representation of the foreign perfection is more strong than that of our own proper deficiences ; for it is very possible to feel a sensation of delight while we contemplate the excellences and the rare qualities of others, though few men are endued with a sufficient portion of philosophy to be pleased with ruminations on the contrary qualities inherent in their own persons. When veneration is pure and unmixed, it will be then able to preserve the place

I have assigned it amongst the agreeable sensations of the heart : but the epistolary form does not require a method so rigorously exact as a systematical work. You will therefore, I hope, give me every latitude in my attempts to express my sentiments.

The delineation of almost every passion or feeling of the human soul has so many imperceptible variations, or, as the French term them, *nuances*, that the difficulty of a precise definition is almost incredible. The assistance of a candid mind is every where requisite for the completion of a work so replete with obstacles. Pardon me this digression. In presence of an object which inspires us with veneration, not only the muscles of the eyebrows, the mouth, and the cheeks become less firm, but the same thing happens to the whole body, particularly the head, the arms, and the knees. When the Orientials cross the hands upon the bosom, whilst the body is inclined, doubtless it is their intention to indicate, by this peculiar trait, the cordiality and depth of the sentiment with which they are affected ; and in clasping their arms strongly against the body they seek to express fear, which commonly relates as well to that as veneration. The reason of this is easy to define ; while we compare a foreign strength with our own weakness, and it is impossible for us to avoid shame every time we have occasion to dread lest the more perfect being should be *sensible* of our weakness.

These are the two sentiments which enforce a tendency towards separation and removal, which are already founded on the very nature of veneration; for he who is penetrated with it imagines himself unworthy a more intimate commerce with a being who appears superior to him in merit: in the like manner, on the other hand, is the proud man affected towards the being he considers as beneath him.

The former removes himself to a certain distance, and the space he places between himself and the object of his veneration becomes the visible symbol of their moral difference.

The affections of pride and veneration encounter each other in this one single expression; but this resemblance is only exterior, for there is a total difference between the intention or the the secret motive of the gesture proper to the one and the other.   In one of your former letters you express a doubt whether the lowering of the body is the expression of veneration adopted by all nations, polished as well as barbarian.   I did

not then penetrate your opinion, but I *now* perceive that, according to *you,* some little people
existing in a retired corner of the globe, or hid in
a remote island, may make an exception to a general rule—and you certainly had the little amiable and interesting nation of Otaheite in your
mind, or I am very much mistaken.*   I grant
that Hawksworth mentions the custom of uncovering the upper part of the body to the
haunches as the expression of veneration adopted
by this people.

It is probable that this nudity designated
frankness and innocence : one party uncovered
their bodies to prove that they concealed nothing hurtful or mischievous.   However this may
be, the origin and signification of the ceremony
we are now speaking of are involved in too much
shade and obscurity to be capable of affording
any reasonable ground of objection against the
universality of a gesture common to all the other
known nations.   Love contemplates a foreign

* From the moment that they were seen afar off (the young
heir presumptive and his sister), Oberea, and many persons
attending, uncovered their heads and the upper parts of their
bodies to the haunches, and thus went before them : consequently, the action of uncovering the body is, according to
all appearances, a sign of veneration and respect among these
people.

perfection in a manner different from veneration. Simple, corporeal beauty excites in us a sentiment soft, tender, and appertaining to love. Love, properly so called, which it is necessary to distinguish from this gross passion which attracts the two sexes, chiefly attaches itself to the qualities of the soul, particularly those of the heart, and gives the preference where mental accomplishment as well as personal perfection immediately flatter the mind in an agreeable manner. When the charms of the form are united to these qualities, when this all-powerful magnet which draws one sex to the other, or when the tenderness of parents towards their children, which belongs to this paramount feeling, associate themselves, then doubtless the sentiment rises to its highest pitch, and its expressions become more eloquent and more animated. Even solid perfections, more dear to the mind than to the heart, may give birth to love; but the expression of this passion then assumes the vague appearance of a satisfaction tranquil and serene. We should do better, then, in opposing this sentiment, under the name of friendship and benevolence, to the other sentiment more characteristically marked, which is distinguished by a languor, a softness, and a tenderness which are peculiar to *it* alone.

An English philosopher has spared me the trouble of painting the expression of this senti-ment for you.

He says, " While we have under our eyes those objects whom we love and who please us, the body, as far as I have been able to observe, takes the following attitude : the head drops a little on one side ; the eyelids are drawn down more close than usual ; the eye, directed towards the object, moves with softness ; the mouth is half opened ; the respiration is slow, and from time to time cut short with a profound sigh, and the arms fall negligently by the side of the body : this is all accompanied with an internal feeling of languor and faintness."

The first and most essential of the propensities of love is that which Aristophanes designates, in his Plutus, by a pleasant fiction, but nevertheless very rich in idea ; *i. e.* the propensity of reunion and community, which, during the most perfect harmony of souls, often acquires such a degree of force that if, according to the expression of the comic Greek, Vulcan should descend from heaven to unite the two lovers as he would join two pieces of iron by the stroke of his anvil at his forge, he would find them already at the height of their wishes.

Lovers, in grasping hands, or in embracing, yield to this soft propensity : it is this penchant which attracts them. Whilst embracing each other, they unite their glowing cheeks and ardent lips, and mutually passing the arms round the neck, alternately repose on the bosom of each other. Sublime and pure friendship, disengaged from each erratic affection, likewise gives testimony of its internal contentment, its desire of a reciprocal communication of souls, its harmony of sentiments, of its wishes for a union, by the clasping of hands, by the embrace, or by the other modes adopted by the various inhabitants of several countries.

To shake the given hand is an expression usual in friendship, benevolence, and salutation. This gesture is rich in signification, for the hand is the tongue of hearty good will. The mind of man, naturally desirous of some symbol or sententious gesture to utter the affections of love, manifestly sets forth this disposition by the pressing language of the hand ; the hand is the general instrument

of the mind.   Pindar placed the heart and hand
as relatives under one and the same parallel.
As it is treason to shake hands with the king, the
only familiarity allowed is to kiss the hand upon
certain occasions.   However in the Chronicle of
Sir Richard Baker, it appears the king made use
of that expression of welcome to his nobles when
they appeared at Westminster.   Persons to this
day apologise when they shake hands with their
gloves on, and sometimes conclude with this elegant witticism; " Excuse my glove, perhaps it
is the more honest skin of the two."   Shaking
hands by common consent is also the natural
gesture of reconciliation.   There are so many
expressions in shaking the hand by which we
discover the disposition towards us that it is
conceived a king ought not to take advantage
of it.   If the hand be pressed very hard, it is an
insinuation of love and forgiveness of injuries:
this pressure is the overture to love; when the
tongue falters to pronounce, the hand insinuates.
This gesture is too feelingly known to require a
more detailed history of it.

The native of *Madagascar*, ignorant of the
more animated expressions of friendship, contents himself with placing his own hand in that
of his friend, without either squeezing it or em-

bracing him : and the islander of *New Zealand*, when he wishes to prove his benevolence, presses his nose against that of his friend, as we Europeans join our lips or hands in the expressions of love and friendship.

A second propensity equally natural and characteristical of love is that which leads us to ameliorate the lot of the object of our affection, to augment its perfections, and place it in the most advantageous light ; to acquire by these obligations new rights upon its affection and benevolence, or to give, by this means, more power to the qualities which are most dear to us.

Whilst I am speaking of love, I ought to add a reflection on the modifications that the intuitive affections, as well as the desires, borrow from their object.

Love, for instance, has a characteristical propriety whilst it consists in a fervent piety, or in a concentrated contemplation of any agreeable object of the imagination ; which, far from being really present to the exterior senses, is not even so supposed to be by the mind. The apple of the eye, hid behind the eyelids, with a look not directed towards any fixed point, which is consequently less brilliant, and appears to be concentrated in the interior, whilst (as we may say) a sombre cloud covers the eye : these are the most remarkable traits of this shade, traits which finish by becoming in the long run a permanent character in the physiognomy of such an enthusiast, or devotee, constantly occupied with similar ideas.

When traits of overwhelming grief unite themselves to those I have just been speaking of, the eye, sad and dim, then announces an interior and mystical suffering, an imagination which feeds in secret on ideas of an exalted but at the same time of a sad and melancholy species. I could say much more on the subject of devotion and enthusiasm, but we have still many matters to treat of, which demand the preference.

LETTER XX.

On the Expression of the disagreeable intuitive Affections—
Of those occasioned by the unfavourable Opinion of others
—Of Contempt and Shame.

THE sketch of love, which I traced for you in my
last letter, then appears incomplete to you ? and,
according to your idea, I should not regard this
affection as the soft sentiment of a happy man ;

> Cui placidus leniter afflat amor.
> > *Tibullus.*

But rather as the bitter and dolorous sensation
of the wretch whose repose it ruins ;

> Quem durus amor crudeli tabe peredit.
> > *Virgil.*

You doubtless forget, my friend, that we are
now only examining the *agreeable* affections, and
that we have not even wished to consider more
than their pure and simple expressions, as well
as their more determinate and characteristical
shades ; of course, if that of mournful love,

wretched and ready to abandon itself to despair, takes the entire expression of the other affections, or at least participates with them in a very intimate manner, I have not done wrong in making mention of it, particularly here.   I might likewise, according to my own ideas, pass over *esteem* in silence; for the expression of this sentiment, as will be proved by a slight inspection of the drawing of Le Brun, has no proper and distinguishing character.   Borrowed from *veneration*, it is solely rendered more moderate, and a certain frank though modest assurance there assumes the place of respectful fear.

Let us commence the examination of the intuitive *disagreeable* affections, by the sentiments which are opposed to pride and veneration, namely, *contempt* and *shame*.   The first of these sentiments consists in dragging others down below our own level ; in conceiving a more lofty idea of our persons and our faculties than of those of another individual: the second consists in humbling ourselves in the opinion of others, by finding that any of our failings or imperfections are known to them.   If to this humbling of ourselves we attach the idea that the ill opinion of another person may have any disagreeable influence upon our happiness, then these sentiments are no longer

pure ones, although they do not absolutely
change their nature. Fear mingles with hate
—hate and malevolence mix with disdain.   I
ought to warn you that we are here only considering pure expressions, and that consequently
I, in this place, only speak of disdain and shame,
inasmuch as disadvantageous opinions, merely
without the concomitant idea of any hurtful or
real influence, is the origin of it.

The play of *disdain* is the overflowing of
pride ; all the difference between these two sentiments is, that the latter is more occupied with
the personal *perfections*, and the former with the
defects of another.   The other marks of disdain
are the turning away from a person, or looking
at him aside, darting a quick glance with a
haughty air.   Sometimes with the head turned
over the shoulder, as if the object were unworthy
of a more serious or attentive examination.   It
often happens that the expression of disgust is
superadded, by a turning up of the nose, and a
slight elevation of the upper lip.   And when the
despised object seems to entertain too high an
opinion of himself, and wishes to oppose pride
against our judgment, the eye then measures him
with the glance of raillery, while the head inclines
a little on one side, as if, on account of our height,

we found a difficulty in comprehending all the *littleness* of our opponent. The shoulders rise, a disdainful smile, mixed with pity, announces the contrast we feel between our own imaginary grandeur and his real insignificance.

If the objects which excite our disdain are not thinking beings but inanimate objects (though these things are not often despised, save as they have a connexion with certain persons), we express the little interest they excite, by an action of repulsing or throwing them away from us; and we apply these expressions, *figuratively,* to moral objects, ideas, sentiments, characters, &c. &c. One of the most sensible expressions of contempt is to neglect the speaker, and to treat with indifference his person, his feelings, and his actions, either by remaining in a perfect state of tranquillity, or by amusing ourselves with more trifling occupations, so as to make him imagine we have forgot his person and all that concerns him so entirely as not even to be sensible of his being present. This indifference becomes so insupportable that the man grows outrageous. For to lose a point after having strained every nerve to obtain the end, and to be robbed of it in the most mortifying manner, in not being able to gain the slightest degree of attention, is a kind of annihilation not only of merit but of existence itself. Hence comes that forcible effect from a contrast, when one actor tranquilly continues his occupation, whether in folding a letter, taking snuff, or adjusting his dress, or humming a lively air, whilst his adversary, transported with rage, is ready to tear himself to pieces.

The play of shame is variable, like that of contempt, according to the difference of circumstances. Sometimes, for example, it is expressed in sudden flight, sometimes in keeping its post in a resolute mode, as the one step or the other seems most calculated to mask a discovered weakness. The nymph surprised at the bath flies, with light foot and garments huddled up in haste, towards the approaching bower, to escape the curious glances of the prying Satyr. The man accused of a moral default seeks to hide his weakness, and destroy by his presence the disadvantageous opinion that might be formed of him, and accordingly, as his failing is more or less public, his impudence and dissimulation are proportionably great; as his accuser is more or less powerful, he the more or less manifests his desire to do away an unfavourable judgment, by his confused motions and inarticulate sentences;

or else he avows his impuissance to withdraw himself from a merited affront, by a stiff immovable attitude, accompanied with a mournful silence and all the symptoms of a complete dejection.

You have, no doubt, seen men of dull minds, whom a lively and merited shame have rendered as immovable as statues, till they can neither advance nor recede. The disagreeable sentiment of their weakness being discovered, and augmented each moment by the presence of witnesses, makes them desirous of a speedy retreat; but they are, in the meantime, tormented with the fear of avowing themselves culpable by this flight; they would willingly say something in their own defence, if they did not fear to aggravate the evil by their clumsy excuses, and add new weights to the load of contempt which overpowers them. They are conscious of the ridiculous figure they make; but, after vainly seeking for a relief from their embarrassment, they end with twirling and twisting their clothes, or tormenting the poor hat they hold in their hands: let any one advise them to be gone, and he will perceive that they will obey him with regret, and with slow, unwilling steps; or, without making one motion, will stupidly wait till somebody

comes and pushes them from the place they occupy. This obstinacy, of neither coming to a
confession nor submitting to contempt, lasts as
long as the desire to snatch themselves from this
painful situation, and becomes more stiff and
more obstinate in proportion as their weakness
is more discovered, and the unfavourable opinion
which results from it is manifested in a more decided and less equivocal manner.

The bashful man well knows that the general air of his visage, and particularly the eyes,
express the interior sentiment which agitates him,
in the least doubtful manner.   And, as it is of
consequence not to betray his own vileness, he
strives to hide from each skilful observer those
witnesses which may depose against himself, and
to command his own looks ever ready to divulge
his secret.   From the moment that his weakness
is discovered, and that the observer no longer
entertains a doubt, from that moment his eyes
are fixed to the earth, and his desire for justification has not force enough to make him raise
them up again to the height of the face of his
adversary, and less to that of his eyes.   For,
however great this desire may be, the fear of be-
traying himself entirely masters him.   He should

have an insurmountable repugnance to acquire a complete knowledge of the thoughts of his opposite, who, by the play of his features, should as plainly indicate his *contempt*.

An ugly old coquette does not dread an honest lookingglass so much as a man governed by shame dreads to look upon those eyes where he expects to see all his faults reflected in a manner equally striking and exact. Nothing, then, is so sensible to a man oppressed with shame as the sight of one who appears steadfastly looking at him. He hangs his head on his breast ; his neck stiffens, as it were, to resist any effort to lift up his head ; and he either averts his timid eyes, or conceals them under his eyelids. All these observations demonstrate to the force of evidence the maxim of Aristotle, which says, " Shame is in the eyes."

I shall say nothing concerning *blushing*, which is another physiological expression of shame. You may consult the passage quoted from Aristotle, if you wish to have an exact explanation of it. That which the physiologists state concerning certain concatenations of nerves, which sometimes diversely affect the arteries of the head, and sometimes accumulate or disperse the blood,

may possibly be very true. But that will not resolve the present question :—for it is not now the
argument whether the mechanism of the body
may render redness and paleness possible, or how
they are effected, but why this mechanism is put
in play in the passions. I am glad that the
form of our correspondence and my previous
declaration both dispense me from entering into
researches of this nature.

LETTER XXI.

Expressions of the Affections where the Object is a real Evil—Chagrin—Allusion to the Story of Niobe—On Sufferance—Violent Despair—Romeo—The Expression of Melancholy—Of Grief—Of violent Rage—Where it leads us to make Attacks on our own Persons.

HATRED and disdain, shame and penitence, may be found together; but we can despise without hatred, and feel shame without repentance; that is to say, we may have contempt for the imperfection we perceive in another, but which cannot be hurtful to ourselves or to the persons whom we love, without this evil quality exciting our hatred. And in like manner shame may be felt without contrition, while we see nothing but weakness in our imperfection, of which we are only sorry that other people have too harsh and keen a sense. The disagreeable affections I propose to examine in this letter are of a different nature; they arise from the contemplation of those real evils which disturb our happiness, or may totally destroy it. I only find four which I can select as useful to a comedian—two of which belong to the cause, and the other two to the sentiment of the evil.

The two first of these affections, which relate to the cause of the evil, are only mute desires which we hide, of which we arrest the activity, and which we, perhaps, only perceive in a confused manner. They prompt us to attack the object which inspires them, or to detach ourselves from it by an effort. Fear, properly so called, does not always give birth to them ; a sort of esteem, accorded to him who offends us, influences our sentiments : sometimes the regard we owe to ourselves makes an impression on our mode of thinking; but we are likewise often governed by other considerations, entirely different, founded on the contempt, esteem, or attachment which we possess for the person of whom we have to complain. When a man is vexed by a woman whom he loves, when a person, illustrious from his rank or qualities, finds himself insulted by a person of inferior requisites, both of them command that anger which is ready to burst out ;—the one for the love of his companion, the other not to compromise with himself ; and both of them, in thus struggling against their anger, which they concentre or smother in the

interior of their souls, may turn pale and tremble as if they were really seized with fear.   This
sentiment may be expressed by the word *vexation*, a denomination which marks this medley of
choler and I know not what, of which I search
in vain for the proper term.   You have found,
in my former letters, the description of the exterior modifications of this affection, particularly
in some of the passages which I have borrowed
from several of the best authors and most
esteemed philosophers.   *Chagrin* is a name which
has been sometimes applied to this sentiment; a
denomination with which I am not satisfied, because it does not indicate the essence of this affection, and its variation from those which are
opposed to it, with sufficient exactitude.

The word *chagrin* does not express, like that
of *vexation*, the connexion with the cause of the
disagreeable sensation; since, whether fearful or
indulgent, *chagrin* leads us to avoid the object
which gives rise to it, whilst vexation rather disposes us to approach, and even to *attack* it.   I
call to mind, still, that this last sentiment changes
itself into hatred when a moral being is recognised as the cause of an unhappy situation; but
the action of this hatred has nothing peculiar in
it except that, whilst in the presence of the hated

object, the fierce look rests on it while the body turns away with a movement of choler.

I am obliged to enter into more wide details concerning the two other kinds of disagreeable affections which are connected with the sentiment of evil. I call them sufferance, and dejection or melancholy : sufferance is an unquiet and active affection, manifesting itself by the tension of the muscles ; it is an interior struggle of the soul against a painful perception, and an effort to surmount and get rid of it. Dejection, or melancholy, on the other hand, is a weak and passive affection : it is a total relaxation of the powers ; a mute and tranquil resignation, without resistance either against the cause or even the sentiment of the evil. The cause of the evil is either superior to us, or cannot be repulsed. Thus we wish not for, or, to speak more fitly, we *cannot* think of vengeance. The sentiment of evil has already tired our resistance and weakened our powers—consequently has lost its violence.

To hold forth the hands together is the expression of those who plead, submit, and resign themselves up with supplication into the power of another. This gesture puts aside any doubts that may exist as to the priority of language between the tongue and the hand ; before a child can lisp its father's name, he is gratified by beholding its little arms stretched out to him, pleading to be taken to his paternal embrace.

To insert the fingers between each other, the hands being upon the lap, is the sluggish expression of those who have fallen into a melancholy muse : to the signification of this gesture accords the oration of Sextus Tullius unto Sulpitius Dictator : " You, our General, deem us, your army, to be handless, heartless, and armourless ; for what else may we think of it, that you, an old experienced Captain, a most valiant warrior, should sit, as they say, with one hand in another, doing nothing ?" Hence Erasmus, " Manibus compressis sidere ;" for this gesture is thought to have a tacit force to damp the lively spirit of mirth and friendly communication. The placing one hand upon another was ever held unlucky. Wilkie, with a masterly feeling, has portrayed this gesture in his excellent picture of Distraining for Rent.

The first sentiment of *Niobe,* when deprived of her children, was *stupor;* the second, the fury of grief carried to the height ; the third was only dejection or melancholy ; for the gods, moved with pity, did not change her to stone till after her return to her country.

Cicero is of opinion that this fiction of the metamorphosis of Niobe is meant to indicate the lasting silence of grief.

" Niobe fingitur lapidea, propter æternum, credo, in luctu Silentium,"—*Tuscul. Quest. L. 3, b.* 26.

Compare Ovid's Metamorphoses, L. vi. Fable 3, v. 303, 309.

Diriguitque malis.

" —————————Lumina mœstis
Stant immota genis : nihil est in imagine vivi—
Nec flecti cervix, nec brachia reddere gestus,
Nec pes ire potest."

Perhaps no passage in all Ovid can exceed this for its pathos and poetical expression.

The explanation of Cicero seems natural enough to be adopted : let us see if it may not be possible to find one more suited to the art of gesture. It appears to me that fixity, or want of motion, is a quality which the aspect of a *rock* impresses more easily on thought than the idea of *silence*—and that a grief, deep and full, such as a mother so cruelly robbed of her children ought to represent, should in fact be motionless: she is totally plunged in the representation of her afflicting fate; and as the soul fixes (as we may say) with a haggard eye on this solitary idea, the whole body (following an analogy explained in former letters) preserves also a fixed and single attitude.

Insensibility is another term of comparison, which does not appear less just to me; for a melancholy, deep and abandoned to mournful ideas, is indifferent to every thing which surrounds it; it regards neither the actions nor the discourse of another person. Some of the beautiful situations of Clementina, in Sir Charles Grandison, will explain this better than any examples which I can borrow from the theatre. The commencement of this immobility, and insensibility, which takes place when melancholy has reached its highest pitch, announces itself from the first by a sort of coldness, and by what the French express so admirably in the term *nonchalance.* Every thing languishes in the melancholy man: the head, heavy and feeble, reclines on the part of the body near the heart; all the points of the dorsal spine, the neck, the arms, the fingers, and the knees are quite relaxed; the cheeks are discoloured, and the eyes directed towards the object which raises the sad-

ness; or, if it is absent, the looks are directed towards the earth, and the whole body bends—

Ad humum mœror gravis deducit.
                    Horace.   De Art. Poet.

The mótion of every member is tardy and
without force or spirit, the step is embarrassed,
heavy, and so dragging, one could almost think
that cords were attached to the legs to impede
them in the performance of their functions.—All
the expression of the other sentiments, especially
the sympathetic ones, lose their elasticity.   The
desire of pleasing ceases with the interest which
we no longer take in the objects which environ
us.   The exterior will be neglected—as Hamlet,
overwhelmed with sorrow, is seen by the lovely
Ophelia—(vide Ophelia's speech to her Father,
act. ii. scene i.) or like the costume of Antiphi-
lus, according to the description given of it by
Śyrus—

    —— —— " offendimus
Mediocriter vestitam veste lugubri.
Sine auro ornatam, ut quæ ornatur sibi,
Nulla mala esse re expolitam muliebri:
Capillus passus, prolixus, circum caput
Rejectus negligenter."
                    Terence, Heautontim ii. *Scen.* iii

To these traits add the paleness of the cheeks, and the aching forehead, often lightly sustained by the hand; the eyes covered, in this attitude, by the fingers; the love of solitude and seclusion; the opened mouth; the slow and silent respiration, interrupted from time to time by deep-fetched sighs, and you will be able to form the idea of melancholy with a variety of shades, differing in some instances, yet, when taken together, bearing a strong resemblance to each other.

You will no doubt spare me the labour of giving the explanation of these traits; we comprehend them all very easily. While examining the very nature of this affection, particularly with their analogy to the man abandoned to sorrow, who loves to attach himself to a single representation, of which the ideas slowly proceed from one characteristical sign to another, and who (from a kind of softness attached to sadness) completely and voluntarily gives up all resistance to the sentiment of sadness with which his soul is overwhelmed.   *(See Plate* XXX.)

You will find all this quite differently expressed in the affection of sufferance.   Here the miens and movements reveal inquietude, and the interior combat of the soul with the dolorous sentiment of evil. The man who suffers is no longer weak and feeble, like the melancholy man ; he is oppressed, he is rent with agonies; the angles of the eyebrows are elevated upwards to the wrinkled forehead ; all the muscles of the face are convulsed and in motion ; the eye is full of fire, but this fire is vague and wandering; the step is wild and heavy; the body is lengthened :—it stretches out as if it had an attack to sustain; the head is raised towards Heaven, with an imploring and supplicating expression; the shoulders are raised up with a violent contraction (an easy motion, consequently very common to the slightest degree of sufferance, such as pity and ironical complaint); all the muscles of the arms and feet stiffen themselves ; the shut hands, which clasp themselves with force, are unclosed, and sometimes, in returning, droop by the side of the body, deprived of all tension : when, at length, tears inundate the visage, they are not full, round, and trickling slowly down the cheeks —they are not the soft, silent tears of melancholy, which issue from the full and relaxed vessels: it is a torrent which a visible commotion of the whole machine, convulsive shocks of the whole visage, press out from the lachrymal glands.

Sufferance being by its nature so active and so unquiet, you will easily comprehend that, in its more slight attacks, the man who suffers ought to deliver himself to indeterminate movements; and agitating himself in every sense on his seat, he will dart up, following irregular directions; sometimes he will vaguely wander, tormented by a secret anxiety: the individual who suffers resembles the sick man who, feeling an uneasiness in every situation, hopes to find comfort from change of place; he turns from one side to the other, and shifts his posture a thousand ways without finding the relief he is so anxious to obtain.   When the sufferance amounts to despair, then these irregular movements, the effects of interior anxiety, become violent.   In this deplorable state the man throws himself on the ground, rolls on the dust, rends his hair, and tears his breast and forehead.   Vide Romeo and the Friar.

> Thou canst not speak of what thou dost not feel:
> Wert thou as young as I, an hour but married,
> Juliet thy wife! Tybalt murdered!
> Then mightst thou rave, then mightst thou tear thy hair,
> And fall upon the ground, as I do now,
> Taking the measure of an unmade grave.

To wring the hands is also a natural expres-

sion of excessive grief, used by those who con-
dole, bewail, and lament. When Heliodorus, the
hated favourite of the Emperor Valens, was dead,
and his body carried forth to be buried, Valens
commanded that many should attend on foot
bareheaded, and some hand in hand, with fingers
clutched, that nothing might be wanting in the
formality of sorrow. " I have never," says Mr.
Sharpe, " beheld this gesture without the most
sensible emotion : even at the theatre I have repeatedly seen this expression from ladies who
witnessed Mrs. Siddons's excellent acting." Of
this gesture Sir Joshua's Count Ugolins is a
splendid example.

Cleopatra and Œdipus were both the authors
of their own misfortunes : they turned their
hands against themselves in the same fury with
which anger avenges an injury. Ought we not
then to suppose that the choler excited by their
own proper follies armed their hands to punish
them for their commission ? But we have seen
that when even no idea of penitence takes place,
and the man is fully satisfied of the justice of his
cause, he also wreaks his fury upon himself for
want of the proper object of his vengeance : we
thus see why, in violent and insupportable sufferings, the same effect takes place, without the

man's being animated with passion against himself nor against others.   Against whom, in effect,
does the widow direct her transport when, standing by the tomb of a beloved husband, and agonized by the recollection of the loss she has sustained, she tears her hair in all the vehemence of
woe ? Notwithstanding, a certain degree of uniformity in the *effects* presupposes the same thing
in the *cause;* and to what common cause can
we attribute the violences by which repentance,
vengeance, and grief determine a man to exercise fury upon himself? According to my own
opinion, in each of these cases, they are only ex-
plosions of grief, the efforts of the soul, by which
she seeks to free herself from the disagreeable
memory of an evil as well as from the insupportable sensations caused by the physical effects of
this idea.

This last circumstance appears demonstrated
to me, because the head, forehead, breast, cheeks,
and sides are exposed to the attack which is
made then precisely on those parts in which the
passions most cause a fermentation of the blood,
and where they create the most powerful emotions
in the nervous system.   It seems as if the soul
sought to appease the interior tumult of the
blood, in letting it flow; and even then the desire

it entertains to comfort itself creates a new pain, because satisfied with too much impetuosity.

This pain nevertheless produces a good effect, because it for some time turns aside the attention from the more insupportable evil, by directing it towards another of a different nature. The critique of Bion had, therefore, more of spirit than of solidity, when the action of Agamemnon, who in the Iliad rends his hair, appeared to him ridiculous and misplaced. It is certain that it is not by a bald head that we sooth sorrow, but the attention is diverted by the act of despoiling the hair.

" Hinc ille Agamemno Homericus et idem Accianus, Scindens dolore identidem intonsam comam."

" In quo facetum illud Bionis, perinde stultissimum Regem in luctu capillum sibi evellere, quasi calvitio moeror larvaretur."

But you will ask me what plausible reason can be alleged, why the inhabitants of Otaheite think they cannot give a greater token of joy, at the return of a beloved object, than tearing the hair or wounding the head and body? It is thus that the mother of Omai acted. According to my judgment, these violences, exercised by a person on himself, are (as in choler) nothing but efforts to give vent to a sensation of an immoderate and disagreeable nature.

Is not boundless joy a kind of sufferance for a polished European, whose blood is less boiling, and whose passions are, generally speaking, much more tranquil? Does not the tumult, thus excited, often even occasion fainting? Notwithstanding, if we reflect on the violence of a people half savage, where the passions, like a blast of wind, compensate for the brevity of their duration by their intenseness,—if we take such circumstances into consideration, I say, what explosion of immoderate joy should surprise us? Travellers remark, that the visage of the inhabitants of *Otaheite* offer expressions of all the affections of the soul infinitely more strong than those we remark upon our own physiognomies.

It is natural, therefore, to conclude, that their passionate actions are determined by a blood so overboiling and impetuous that it is difficult for us to form an idea of its effects.

I have been speaking of the disagreeable affections in the same manner that I made mention of the agreeable ones; in taking them in the superior degree, where their expression is most eloquent and most strong. I have, in the mean time, endeavoured to paint such as are pure and simple. The examination of their different shades, belonging to the theory of composed expression, will be considered hereafter : motives, which you will no doubt approve, oblige me to pass them over in silence at the present.

LETTER XXII.

The Answer of Garrick to a French Comedian—Of Intoxica-
tion—Preservation of Character.

GARRICK thus answered a French comedian who
asked his opinion of the manner in which he had
performed a character in a certain play : " You
have acted the part of a drunkard with much
fidelity, which is extremely difficult to be effected in such little parts; but permit me to
make one slight critique—your left leg was too
sober."

Upon various occasions I should be tempted
to make the same remark to a number of players.

" According to my weak judgment, you have
done ample justice to such or such a situation
(for I can rarely hazard the *tout ensemble* of a
character); you have perfectly imitated the intoxication of the passion you had to imitate; but
your foot, your hand, your eye, your neck, your
mouth (or any other part I chanced to find defective) was too tame."

Do not you think, like me, that a similar extent of Garrick's criticism would be in effect well founded? Since the physical intoxication attacks the whole nervous system, from the top of the head to the bottom of the feet, the same thing should, I think, take place in the moral intoxication of the affections: for the man has but one soul, which modifies the whole body. Thus, when a simple affection directs all the forces of the soul towards one single point, and the ideas and sentiments are in perfect unison, then the whole body ought to partake of the expression, and every member to cooperate with it.

It is necessary then, that the actor, while studying his character, should not content himself in general reflections upon each passion, but give himself much trouble to learn what part of his body may contribute to its effect: if any of his powers are defective, he ought to correct them either by his own observation or by the judgment of his friends who, if his self love does not repulse each salutary counsel, will generally be both able and willing to instruct him.

It is not only requisite that the most perfect harmony should exist between all the members of the body and every trait of the countenance to give the expression of the sentiment, but it is

also necessary that this harmony should be pro-
portioned to the degree of force and vivacity
which the sentiment requires.   If *desire* manifests itself too much by the play of the arms, and
too little by that of the feet; if fear does not
sufficiently *open* the eyes and the mouth while
the body staggers, and the lifted arms remain
immovable ; if *anger* does not impress the deep
frown on the forehead, or leaves the lip tranquil
while the foot stamps with rage, the whole illusion is put to sudden flight, and the actor still
lingers after the character has vanished out of
sight.

LETTER XXIII.

On the Rule of complete Expression.

I GRANT that you have reason, when you say that my remarks on perfect harmony in the delineation of a character are adapted chiefly to such actors as may perhaps never find any occasion for their practice: it is nevertheless certain, that some performers, not of the best, nor even of the mediocre rank, but those who, in their own judgment, possess the most accomplished talent, sometimes commit the most palpable absurdities. Did you ever see the musical entertainment of Selima and Azor, founded on the pretty tale of Beauty and the Monster? When the father of Selima is excusing himself for having gathered the enchanted rose, he approaches the Monster with all the assurance and familiarity of a man who knows very well that his dear friend and tavern companion is hid behind the ugly mask.

That is villanous. Actors who commit such gross mistakes as this must be deprived of that feeling in their art which is essentially necessary to carry it to perfection; which, if refused by nature, can never be supplied by any rules of art: the rules of arts, in general, are not like moral laws, destined to the *worst*, but for the *best* subjects.

But I am again wandering into digressions, which I ought to avoid with care, since your objections and remarks too frequently make me wander from my route. To return to my subject then.

Hope, gratitude, pity, suspicion, desire, envy, clemency, and many other sentiments most surely are not deficient in their proper expression; yet all these affections, you tell me, are not, hitherto, characterised by any particular trait. The difficulty is serious; but have a little patience—let us speak of gratitude in the first instance. It is impossible to characterise this affection by proper and individual traits; and if it is not demonstrated simply, as love or as veneration, it is then necessary that it should adopt some intermediate shade, common to each of these two sentiments. Pity can only be expressed in the composed play of bounty and of sufferance; envy can only distinguish itself from hatred and sufferance by the accessary desire of hiding itself from all eyes, and by the downcast and furtive glance of shame, which, in a soul however insensible, always accompanies this base and contemptible passion. Suspicion will only betray itself in adding to the expression of chagrin, the anxious regard of curiosity, and listening to all conversations from which any thing may be discovered.

To put forth the right hand spread open is the gesture of bounty, liberality, and a free heart: thus we reward and bestow our gifts: hence to open the hand in the Hebrew phrase implies to be free hearted, munificent, and liberal. Pliny observes, that the Greeks called the span, or space from the thumb to the little finger's end, *dorow*, which it is not unlikely is the reason that gifts in the Greek language are called *dora*, because they are presented with the hand. A commentator on the text " Let not thy left hand know what thy right hand doth," informs us that it is a symbolical expression like the hieroglyphics of the Egyptians: the right hand is open, free, and manifestly put into action; therefore the right hand denotes liberality, whereas the left hand is of a contrary nature. Our courts of law forbid any one giving his left hand, who is about to make an affidavit, and ordains " that the person

who makes an affidavit shall lay his right hand
upon the book." Hogarth's genius would not
let this circumstance escape him in his picture of
Industry and Idleness, where the idle apprentice
is brought before the industrious one: the wretch
who has turned evidence against his accomplice
is taking the oath with his left hand laid upon
the book instead of the right. It is said, the
dealers in perjury at Westminster Hall, as well
as at the Old Bailey, consider this little circumstance as a complete salvo for false swearing. In
another picture, the polling for a member of parliament, Hogarth humorously makes a dispute
between two barristers as to the legality of an
oath : an old soldier has lost a leg, an arm, and
a hand, and has laid upon the book an iron
which is fastened to a wooden arm : the effect is
truly ludicrous, and according to the letter of
the law would admit of much quibbling.

Clemency can only become visible whilst the
amiability of bounty is tempered by the coldness
of pride ; which, in descending from the pinnacle
of its grandeur, allows another sentiment to develope itself. *Envy*, by its nature, partakes of
hatred, and can only be delineated by the expression of that passion. Lastly *Hope*, which
only views bliss in the future, is not always free

from *fear ;* she can only then depict herself in one point of view; the traits of the visage must take an expression of desire, with a mixture of *joy* and *fear.* Thus you see the impossibility of being so very, very distinct as you seem to require.

He who has studied the effects which each affection produces by the modification of the traits of the visage and the motions of the body, and has remarked, at the same time, by what peculiar parts of the frame each passion expresses itself, will without difficulty perceive by what mode different and various sentiments may unite in one single expression; and how, for example, the sufferings of a lover, who is occupied with the idea, at once voluptuous and sad, of his absent mistress, may be expressed by the play of the physiognomy. *Sufferance* principally affects the *superior* part, and the voluptuous sensation of love the *inferior* part of the face: of course, if the first sentiment be only a shade, the interior angles of the eyebrows will elevate themselves in a manner almost imperceptible, and will cast a *very slight* shadow on the forehead, which will be produced by a wrinkle, &c. On the contrary, we shall behold the soft smile of love playing around the *mouth,* whilst the eye, languishing and turned towards the object, will partake of each of these sentiments. On the contrary, if the pleasure be only a shade of the sufferance which predominates, the principal expression will be found upon the forehead, and the wandering smile upon the cheek and lip will become more feeble. In this latter mixture we also remark more of tension in the muscles of the rest of the body, and in the former more of softness and relaxation.

In searching for examples to unfold in detail all the possible shades of different gestures in each class of expressions, I regard it as so easy a thing to indicate that which is proper to a determinate mixture of sentiments that the labour almost appears totally superfluous. It is often, without doubt, difficult to find the veritable mixture of passions, as well as the just proportions, for every case; but this is not the concern of the theoretician, who solely determines the expression of the given sentiments. This case concerns the actor, who, in studying his character, ought to enter thoroughly into it. And this likewise concerns the metaphysician. The comedian, who is willing to examine his art like a man of sense, and not from pure instinct, ought, surely, to consider something else beside the theory of gesture.

If the problem given be to reunite the expression of two opposite desires which encounter in the soul, I maintain that, to resolve them, it is sufficient to know these two desires, and also their proper and characteristical expressions. To know if these desires are in equilibrio, or if either predominate; and, lastly, to ascertain the degree of preponderance, after which it will not be difficult to find the veritable expression which will indicate completely, and in a striking manner, the affection by which the soul is governed in a given situation. The desire of Hamlet to discover the terrible secret of his family is very preponderant in his soul at the moment he follows the spectre of his father; yet is this desire somewhat weakened by fear, when an unknown being and the idea of another world take possession of his mind. This weakness augments as the King leaves his companions and approaches the spectre. Thus, when he violently breaks from the arms of his friends, exclaiming,

> By heaven, I'll make a ghost of him
> That lets (hinders) me—

his movement and action ought to be strong and animated: from the time he begins to walk, the step should become slow and moderate, but firm and resolved. Successively he will become more circumspect—he will walk without liveliness, and his body will approach to the vertical position. Nevertheless, that you may not reproach me, because I choose the most easy examples, and neglect those which offer greater difficulties, I beseech you to be so good as to indicate yourself such composed sentiments as you shall judge possible, and I will endeavour to determine the expression of them in a satisfactory manner; or, if you like it better, give me such a possible gesture as may reunite many expressions, and we shall then see how I succeed in developing the general expression.

It may be asked if, in the language of gesture, there are any synonymous movements of the same signification, which may be employed the one for the other?

If a comedian has a desire to arrive at that rigorous exactitude which, in all the arts, constitutes the supreme merit of the artist, ought he not to display the same fine discernment in the choice of his gestures which an able author displays in the selection of his words?

Macrobius reports, that Roscius and Cicero sometimes challenged each other to express the same thought in the most various ways; that is to say, the actor by variety of gesture, the orator by his copiousness of phrase.

Satis constat contendere eum (Ciceronem) cum ipse histrione (Roscio) solitum, utrum ille sæpius eandem sententiam variis gestibus efficeret, an ipse per eloquentiæ copiam sermone diverso pronunciaret. Quæ res ad hanc artis suæ fiduciam Roscium abstraxit, ut librum conscriberet, quo eloquentiam cum histrionia compararet.—*Macrob. Satur.* l. 2. c. 10.

If, as we have good reason to believe, the variations of the one were connected with those of the other, if they were in some sort reciprocal translators—Cicero expounding the gestures of pantomime by words, and Roscius expressing the words of the orator by gestures, this proof will result from it, viz. that the language of gesture has its synonymous terms in the same sense as oral language, and that in both one and the other the same principal idea may be differently expressed, but always with other accessary ideas.

It is difficult to speak of the gesture and mien in general, and particularly of their more delicate shades, in a clear and distinct manner. I shall not be at all surprised, my friend, should many consider these delicate touches as vain subtilties, invented by prejudice or by caprice. Our idea of the art is not yet correct, and we determine on it as the Mussulman judges of music: the instrument which makes the loudest noise is the most agreeable to us, and he who plays on it with most quickness and violence appears to be the greatest virtuoso. Often, while the whole theatre resounds with shouts and acclamations, we are tempted to whisper from the scene the words which Hippomacus the flute-player said to one of his scholars: " Do you think you have played well, because such auditors as *these* have applauded you ?"—*Vide Ælian.*

Clapping the hands is an action indicative among all nations of applause, congratulation, joy, assent, and approbation. Applause is a vulgar note of encouragement. " Populus Romanus," says Cicero, speaking of theatrical applause, " manus suas non in defendu libertate, sed in plaudendo consumit." Applause has been heard in our courts of justice which not even the authority or gravity of the judge could suppress; and as an example of this gesture the reader may be referred to the gallery of a London theatre.

It frequently happens, that while false acting appears brilliant and alluring, it is more admired and applauded than a part less livelily personified, though the latter mode be more adapted to its respective character, and, indeed, the only one which could be assumed with propriety. Novelty is preferred to truth. Our theatre boasts one actress * whom it would be superfluous to name, who never sacrifices propriety for the gratification of temporary applause. Queen Katharine, in Shakspeare's Henry VIII. is a sublime instance of this sort of acting. In the scene of the trial, where all her energies are roused, and on the sick bed, where every faculty is depressed and worn out, all is truth, and there is not one exaggerated trait from the beginning to the end.

Hæc semel placuit decies repetita placebit.

---

* Mrs. Siddons, now retired from the Stage.

LETTER XXIV.

Expression— Painting—Anecdote from Macrobius—Example from Shakspeare—Baron the celebrated French Tragedian.

In your last you demand my answer to an objection which appears important to you.—You say that the invention of the veritable expression for a given affection being so easy, you cannot divine how there can be so much difficulty in the drawing of heads of expression, and so much merit in succeeding in them. But have you reflected on the very great difference which exists between the painter and the actor? The one has merely to modify the features of his own face—the other has to invent the face and all, besides the difficulty of conforming to all the rules and principles laid down in the art of physiognomy. Nature aids the one in expressing those passions with which he is affected; the other is forced, by the process of art, to exhibit, on a plain surface, the most happy object his imagination has been able to select out of a thousand.

I shall presently explain myself more clearly upon this subject, after I shall have terminated the important researches which I propose to place at the end of the theory of expression. The matter is, to know when it is permitted to make use of painting in the play of the gestures.

In order to prepare ourselves for the proper treatment of this question, let us, before every thing else, propose the examination of a few examples. I should have wished to have borrowed the first from the theatre of ancient Rome ; but I have found that the application would hardly be allowable.

You will doubtless be of my opinion, when you consider the fact such as Macrobius relates it, and not in the way it is recounted by some modern writers, after that author. Hylas, the scholar of Pylades, and almost sufficiently advanced in his art to rival his master, one day played, or, following the expression of the ancients, danced a piece, of which the last words were—*The great Agamemnon !*—Hylas, to express the idea of greatness, stretched out his whole body, as if he meant to indicate the measure of a very great man. Pylades, placed in the middle of the audience, could not contain himself, but cried aloud, " You represent *length*—not *grandeur.*" The

people, excited by this critique, insisted that Pylades should get upon the stage, and act the same
part *himself.* Pylades obeyed; and when he
came to the passage in question, he represented
Agamemnon as pensive; since nothing, in his
opinion, was so characteristical of a great king as
thought for all.

Nec Pylades Histrio nobis omittendus est,
qui clarus in opere suo fuit temporibus Augusti
et Hylam discipulum usque ad æqualitatis con-
tentionem eruditione provexit. Populus deinde
inter utriusque suffragia divisus est, et cum canticum quoddam Saltaret Hylas cujus clausula
erat :

Τον μεγαν Αγαμεμνονα. Sublimem ingentemque
Hylas velut metiebatur, non tulit Pylades et ex-
clamavit è cavea.

Συ μακρον, ε μεγαν ποιεις. Tunc populus eum
coegit, idem saltare canticum. Cumque ad locum
venisset, quem reprehenderat, expressit *cogitan-
tem* nihil magis ratus magno duci convenire quàm
pro *omnibus cogitare.—Saturnal,* l. 2.

According to the manner in which the Abbe
du Bos, and particularly Cahusac, recount this
anecdote, it seems as if Hylas had committed
some very puerile fault, of which, nevertheless, I

do not find any trace in the writings of Macrobius.

It is probable that this fault merely consisted in seeking to express grandeur, merely by the stretching out of the body, and that he thus outraged this expression. A passage from Quintilian will better explain the difference which exists between painting and expression, and how the former is often very faulty. This critic severely interdicts all those gestures with which we imitate those objects which are the subjects of discourse. He adds that, in comedy, those actors who had a portion of reputation observed this rule, although their whole art was confined to imitation, and that the best among them strove rather to express the sense than the words. The rule, such as Quintilian has here fixed it, is not, in truth, too exactly fixed; but the examples he borrows from an oration against Verres are not ill chosen, and their examination will conduct us to a more definitive judgment of this rule. Cicero rallies Verres with the most bitter contempt, because, on account of the departure of the fleet from the port of Syracuse, he was found upon the river, habited like a Greek, and leaning voluptuously on a courtesan. The orator makes him know the horror which his infamous conduct inspired, in having, without sentence, information, or delinquency, caused the Roman citizen Gavius to be beaten to death with rods, in the public market-place of Massina.

" An orator ought not to copy," says Quintilian, " the attitude of Verres, who holds a vile courtesan under his arms ; nor that posture and movement of the arms which demand the action of an executioner; nor the groans and cries which pain wrings from a sufferer."

An indecent softness, fustigation, and the pain of that discipline, were the *objects* of the thought of Cicero : disdain, choler, astonishment, and horror were the sentiments which these objects excited in his soul.   Thus Quintilian desires that we should represent in the tribunal, as on the scene, not the immediate exterior objects which strike the senses, not the foreign sentiments by which we are moved, but the proper and actual sentiment—or, to explain myself otherwise, he wishes us not to express the objects which occupy our thoughts, but the sentiments with which we consider those objects.   It is indifferent whether these objects be things purely corporal, or even the movements of the soul.   To wish to paint the

alarm of Gavius, when dragged to undergo un-
merited punishment, would be as false as to imitate the action of the person fustigating him.   In
all cases, the veritable gesture is that which expresses the sentiment of the moment, and which
exclusively predominates in the mind of the
orator.   I give to this gesture the name of *expression,* and to the other that of *painting.*   The
best determined rule on this head would then be,
that actors and orators ought not to paint actions but express thoughts.

An example will prove the justice of this
rule.   Hamlet, in the act of demanding an
important service of Horatio, prepares him in
a very natural manner, by the compliments he
pays him:

Horatio. O, my dear Lord,—
Hamlet. Nay, do not think I flatter:
For what advancement can I hope from thee,
That no revenue hast, but thy good spirits,
To feed, and clothe thee ? Why should the poor be flatter'd ?
No, let the candied tongue lick absurd pomp ;
And crook the pregnant hinges of the knee,
Where thrift may follow fawning.   Dost thou hear ?
Since my dear soul was mistress of her choice,
And could of men distinguish her election,
She hath seal'd thee for herself : for thou hast been
A man who, suffering all, hast suffer'd nothing ;
A man who Fortune's buffets and rewards
Hath ta'en with equal thanks.

Again :

> Give me that man
> That is not Passion's slave, and I will wear him
> In my heart's core, ay, in my heart of heart,
> As I do thee.—

You doubtless remember the actor, who, in reciting the latter lines of this quotation, really *crooked* the knee, and *kissed the hand* as if he wished to seize and kiss the hem of a purple mantle. This false play struck you at the time, and every man of taste felt as we did.—In reflecting on the contempt which every word of the Prince manifests for the base and groveling spirit of a parasite, and the pains he takes to make Horatio think him far above so despicable a character, how could this actor think of imitating an object of detestation ?—If he wished to demonstrate this passage by a striking gesture, he ought rather to have *elevated* than abased himself. He should have taken the air of spleen and dissatisfaction, and not that of respect, which is its diametrical opposite. He ought rather to have rejected a humiliating thought with the hand than have directed it to earth in a base and servile manner. The following anecdote is related of Baron, the French Æsopus.

Baron, after his retreat, which lasted twenty

years, reappeared upon the stage : it was then a
prey to a parcel of declaimers, who bellowed out
verses instead of reciting them. He reappeared
in the character of Cinna. His simple, majestic,
noble entrance was not at all relished by an audience accustomed to the strut and bounce of
the actors of the day : but when, in the picture
of the conspiracy, he came to the recital of these
verses,

Au seul nom de César, d' Auguste, et d' Empereur,
Vous eussiez vu leurs yeux s'enflammer de fureur ;
Et dans un même instant, par un effet contraire
Leur front pâlir d' horreur, et rougir de colère ;

he was seen to turn successively pale and red ;
the cabal trembled, and held their peace.

This cabal, however, must have been endowed
with slender powers of criticism ; for it was struck
dumb at the precise moment it ought to have
burst forth. But I do not think this anecdote
has any foundation with respect to Baron, or
any other actor ; for suppose that this player
really had an imagination strong enough to have
produced so rapid a succession of physiological
expressions, so contrary and so difficult to represent, we know likewise that, according to the
custom of the French theatre, he must have put

on rouge.—Now how is it possible for him to
have been able to turn so visibly pale and red,
covered as he was with paint? But even if he
had possessed those extraordinary physiological
powers, he must then, according to my judgment, have committed a very gross error:—for
does not Cinna, in this scene, bring a piece of
joyful intelligence to his mistress?—ought he
not to raise her hopes, to animate her courage?
—Now if these sentiments fill up his whole soul,
how could their opposites, *fear* and *rage*, acquire
sufficient power to manifest themselves with so
much violence and rapidity.

These preliminary reflections will, I trust, suffice for the present, more particularly as the subject is too copious to be exhausted in a single
letter.

LETTER XXV.

Of the Reunion of Picturesque and Expressive Gestures—
Where their Union is possible—And where the contrary.

You have doubtless forgotten the contents of many of my former letters, since you ask, Why I have only made a general mention of painting relative to the arts of gesture and theatrical action ? Why I have talked of the possibility of a mixture of gestures picturesque and expressive, whilst I wish to proscribe all imitation of those objects which strike upon the senses, and simply to require those expressions by which the soul is affected ? I shall ask, in my turn, Is it necessary that expression and painting should be always in opposition, without the possibility of union ? May there not be some particular circumstances where they may partly or totally unite ; and are there not others where they are entirely confounded together ? Have I not myself more than once endeavoured to direct your attention towards these objects ? In one of my letters,

speaking of the play of admiration, I have formally said that the expression of the interior
sentiment confounded itself with the painting of
the object offered to the senses ; because, in *admiration*, the soul, entirely occupied with the
representation of its object, strives to assimilate
itself to it, and consequently the expression analogous to her situation becomes of itself the imitation, and the painting of the object.   This
remark has helped me to explain to you why the
admiration of any thing great dilates the breast,
and likewise enlarges the whole body, and occasions an opening of the mouth and eyes ; whilst
the contemplation of a sublime subject occasions
an elevation or rising of the body.   I have also
remarked, that the spectator, strongly affected
and hurried away by the interest which the representation of a theatrical piece excites in him,
imitates the looks, and even the movements of
the actors, by alternately participating their
mirth or their sadness, as long as no personal
and contrary sentiments cross these exterior expressions.   In short, I have begged you to remark, on the subject of moral sympathy, excited
by characters noble, firm, and sublime, or by
actions which announce grandeur, courage, or
philanthropy, that these sentiments awaken in

our soul that noble pride, that warmth of enthusiasm, that soft sensibility of our hero—and that
we adopt the air and imitate the gestures of the
object of our admiration and esteem.—It appears
useless in this place to prove the justice of these
observations, which you have already tacitly acknowledged. It is most certainly a happy circumstance for mankind in general, that the soul
has this strong propensity to the imitation of
great and noble sentiments. It is to this propensity we owe the succession of great men who
have shed a lustre on their families and their
countries.

Were it not for this motive of the human
heart, virtue might expire, and genius be extinguished. Fired with the noble imitation we are
now describing, the son strives to emulate the
virtues of the father; he catches the divine spark
before it can be extinguished, and, like a Phœnix,
rises to nobler heights than even the parent bird
had previously attained. But as every general
rule has an exception, it is needless to state
that it requires more than common powers to
imitate with effect and success. Imitation does
not simply consist in volition; the mind must
be endowed with similar energies. The divinæ
particulum auræ, as the Roman satirist terms it,

is necessary to the full effect of a successful resemblance. To imitate the inherent qualities of
grand and sublime souls must presuppose similar qualities in the imitator : but the external
modifications of the form are by no means so
hard to be seized upon. Before I return to the
main subject of the work, it may be necessary to
say a few words on the subject of mimicry.

Mimicry is a talent which has been very much
descried. In a moral point of view, perhaps, the
practice of this art cannot well be defended : but
surely to the person who can master his manners,
voice, and features, so as to give a faithful representation of those of another person, must
be accorded the praise of ingenuity at least.
Mimicry is connected with the picturesque play.
This may perhaps assist you in the deduction of
the second rule. The picturesque play is the
sole true one, or, at least, is totally irreprehen-
sible, when the design of exciting more lively
ideas of certain objects predominates, or while
the individual sentiment of the interlocutor voluntarily gives place ; because it is only in fulfilling this design he is able to satisfy himself. It
sometimes happens that the play, fitted to the
design, is in perfect harmony with that of the
sentiment, and that there results from it a repre-

sentation so completely faithful that one would believe the sentiments to be homogeneous, and all the soul of the interlocutor, without any distinction of individual self, dissolved in the idea of the object : he finds himself in his case who warmly complains to the judge of an insult committed against his honour and his good name; he imitates, with the greatest vivacity, the proud, insolent tone, the anger and humiliating contempt of him who has committed the offence; not as one would think to give the judge a correct idea of the event, and to convince him of the justice of his complaint, but principally on account of the satisfaction which a similar imitation gives to the passion with which he is inspired; for the insolence, pride, and contempt of his enemy excite the selfsame sentiments in his *own breast*.

There is often a mixture of expression and painting in pantomime, as in painting itself, to his appearance who does not attentively examine it to the bottom, which is only the reunion of several expressions, of which one appears to be painting, because it belongs to the homogeneous sentiment. This is the case of the lover, who, charmed with the majestic shape, the deportment full of grace and dignity, the mingled fire and softness in the glance of his mistress, is so much attached to the representation of these qualities that he endeavours to appropriate some portion of them to himself. He will imitate this noble and majestic carriage; but, maugre this apparently picturesque expression, we shall always recognise the lover in the languor of his looks, his mouth gently half opened, and the fugitive smile which wanders on his lips and on his cheeks—and in this way a kind of bastard mien and gestures are produced, an expression which much resembles that of clemency, because the dignity and pride of the beloved object are there reunited to the tenderness and respectful attachment of the lover.

There are however some cases, where what we call the *painting* will come tardily off, because accidental circumstances will destroy all possibility of illusion. The giant can give no idea of the diminutive figure of the dwarf, nor can the dwarf at all convey the idea of the towering proportions of the giant.

A man who should attempt to copy the manners of a sailor begging in the street might hit off his tone, his look, and his gesture, but the want of the wooden leg would still render the painting deficient.

To make this case more clear to the theatrical connoisseur, I shall demand what he would think of a person going through the part of Sir John Falstaff, striving to hide a lean and meagre figure, by merely thrusting out his stomach and confining his hands? Unless he took some means of giving us the idea of corpulency, the painting would immediately become incomplete. *(See Plate* XXXI.)

It is easy to see that this is not the predicament in which the tutor (mentioned above) found himself placed, whom the return of the same fault, frequently committed by his pupil, had already too much displeased for him to be able, correctly, to imitate his imbecile manner; still, nevertheless, preserving the desire to amend and humiliate him by a representation of his awkward and ridiculous gesture. Here a complete reunion of the imitation with the expression of displeasure is a matter of the greatest difficulty.

It will be necessary, then, by sacrificing of parts, and by reciprocally altering them, to seek their reunion by a middle attitude, which will not be exactly either the one or the other. Our preceptor, then, will render his mouth idiotical, and in this grimace, his lower lip will be pendent, but at the same time it will find itself a little drawn towards the angles of the mouth. His head will fall forward, but with more force; his eyes will stare, while his approaching eyebrows and the wrinkles on his forehead will discover his choler. In a word, all his face will become a veritable caricatura, in which one will clearly observe that, to the imitation of an attitude, which is foreign to him, personal traits of raillery and ill humour will associate themselves.

Neither of the cases which I have been indicating take place when the soul is not so sufficiently occupied in the contemplation of the object that the painting may confound itself with the expression. When the design of rendering the intuitive object does not predominate, and when this design does not support itself with a sensible degree of vivacity on the side of the sentiment which the soul feels, then, not only the pure and simple painting but also the mixture of picturesque play and expression ought to be rejected: for, in all these cases, the painting is in contradiction with the sentiment of the soul, and is neither analogous, physiological, or determined by any design. After these principles, judge yourself, if, in my last letter, I was wrong in blaming the play of the actor in the part of Hamlet, or that of Baron.

The passages in question had no need of any pantomimical commentary to render them intelligible : but where then, you will ask me, *are* the cases where the soul is really entirely occupied with its object ? Where are those where the design of communicating a lively and thinking idea predominates exclusively, and subsists with a force nearly equal to the sentiment ? To those who propose such questions, I shall reply, that they expect from the theory of gesture and theatrical action more than it is capable of affording. It requires instructions so precise and so determinate that, in dispensing the artist from personal study, they reduce him to the simple rank of a mechanic labourer.

In this, the rule can only develope the natural sense with which the artist ought to be endowed, facilitate his means of arriving at clear notions of the different parts of his art, awaken his dormant genius, or recall him from wrong paths, and aid him to resolve doubtful cases with celerity and precision. For the rest, we might yet give some particular instructions; for example, that the actor ought not to allow himself the expression of any idea, or any sentiment which his discourse announces as foreign to his soul: that in metaphors, he ought, above all things, to beware of attaching himself to qualities which, not appertaining to the comparison, have no connexion with the idea nor the sentiment which rules the soul. When Freeport, in the English Merchant, says to the young lady, " Madam, I don't love you at all," would it not be ridiculous should his face express a languishing softness?

Would it not appear pitiable in Marc Antony, if, when recalling to the minds of the Roman populace the circumstance of Cæsar's having rejected the crown which had been offered him, he should describe a circle to represent it in the air? It would be still more ridiculous, if, when calling Cæsar the crown of all heroes, he should make use of the same action. These faults appear so gross that it may be judged superfluous to warn the comedians against their commission: notwithstanding, how many of them are there who, proud of their own taste and their pretended acquirements, fall into errors equally absurd and ridiculous! Have you never heard one of these modern rhapsodists, declaiming bombast nonsense, and gesticulating without intermission, and often representing each figurative expression in so comical a way that it would have puzzled the gravity of a Crassus or a Cato to have kept their countenances?

In the scene of Emilia Galotti *, where Odoardo says to the Countess Orsino, " Weaken not
this drop of poison in a large vessel" (or vul-
garly, a great tub—*tonneau)*, it is visible that he
ought to feel the most lively impatience of desire;
it is equally clear that, in this situation, the play
of the actor ought to express this impatience
solely, and that, consequently, it is quite impossible for him to find sufficient time to indicate
to the countess all that he finds odious in her
conduct by a detailed metaphor.   Nevertheless,
I remember to have seen an actor, in the character of Odoardo (I confess it was at a little
barn, where my curiosity engaged me to stop),
who attempted to make this speech *figurative;*
and can you guess by what means?   An exact
observer of the rule prescribed by Riccoboni, he
lifted up the right arm methodically, and curv_
ing his hand, held it down to the ground, as if
he was pouring something on the earth *(as in
Plate* XXXII).   This play was meant to designate the drop of poison.

After this first gesture, stretching out his
arms, with the fingers widely scattered *(as in*

* The play of Emilia Galotti may be found in the translation of the German Theatre, by B. Thompson, esq. author
of " The Stranger."

Plate XXXIII.) he seemed to wish to embrace something of vast circumference, and this was, according to him, the painting of the *tub.*

Do not think that I insert this anecdote merely to make you laugh. You yourself know an actor who, whilst representing the character of Odoardo, struck himself violently on the belly, with his clenched fist, every time he pronounced the word *tonneau:* and is this fault less ridiculous or more excusable than the former one? This may suffice, my friend, for the rule given by Quintilian, and will, at the same time, serve as an answer to your first question: to wit, if this rule would not banish every sort of lively representation from the scene? In the following epistle, I shall answer to that which concerns the representation of pantomimical subjects.

LETTER XXVI.

Extent of the Rule concerning Pantomime—In what Manner all Painting detrimental to the Expression may be considered, even while the Action forms its Subject—Subjects of Roman Pantomime—Remark on a Passage in Lucian.

AFTER what I have said in the beginning of our correspondence, you will not suspect me of being too much prejudiced in favour of pantomime : notwithstanding you wish me to regard it as a practicable species of theatrical representation ; a species which, from its origin, and since its re-establishment by the celebrated Mr. Noverre, has had the most decided success.   It appears to you then that I cannot dispense myself of speaking concerning pantomimes, since, deprived of words, it is entirely dependant on the art of gesture.   But, according to your opinion, the rule established for the actor cannot extend to pantomime, because that he, according to my own confession, can by no means be exempt from certain signs proper to the figurative painting of the objects of his sentiments.

It appears to me that I ought to have added
to this remark, that pantomime has a real need
for similar signs, whilst it imposes on itself the
necessity of making objects known, of which the
spectators had not any idea; that is to say,
whilst aspiring to the title of the CREATIVE POET,
it wishes to invent its *own subjects*, their intrigues,
and their *denouements;* for, in effect, it is possible that there may be some, where pantomime
may be able to avoid all representation contrary
to the expression.

There are some events in life which, by all
their symptoms, have their characteristical proprieties, which are so commonly known, that
seeing them represented in pantomime, we have
no occasion to ask what object we strive to imitate.   You doubtless recollect that pantomimical farce, at which the English assisted in one
of the islands of the Society in the South Sea,
(Voyage round the World by Foster, vol. 2d.)
which truly could only be represented by a
people as uncorrupted and uncivilized as these
Islanders.   You will also recollect to have read
the description of the warlike dances of the
American savages, in which they represented to
their spectators, in pantomime, all the events

practised in a maritime expedition; the march, the attack, the combat, the manner of taking prisoners, and the retreat.

" He (the dancer) represents the departure of the warriors—the march—he goes in ambush—he makes his approaches—he stops, as if to take breath—then, of a sudden, he grows furious, and one would think he was about to exterminate the whole world: recovered from this excess, he seizes some one of the company, as if making him prisoner of war—he pretends to cleave the head of another; at length he falls to running with all his speed: he frequently stops to recover: this is a retreat, first hasty and then tranquil.   He afterwards expresses, by various cries, the different sensations he had experienced during his last campaign, and finishes with the recital of all the gallant actions he had performed during the war."—*Charlevoix. Hist. de. Nouv. France.*

During the dance, the warrior has the same design as the actor has sometimes upon the stage during his recitations and descriptions, that is to say, he wishes to excite in the souls of his spectators the images of certain objects, in a manner striking and intuitive. In truth, he then paints, but it is with the same sight as the comedian: his representation becomes clear, because every one knows what it is he means to imitate, and because the objects of his imitation reduce themselves precisely to the motions of his body, which serve him as exactly as sight, colours, and contour aid and assist the painter. There is no need of figures of conception but whilst he wishes to design events which are by themselves different from the actions and movement of his body, or when the employment or significations of these are not at all known to the spectators.

The ballets of action of the comic kind, which are generally represented after the pieces of the theatre, are, for the most part, imitations of daily and ordinary events, which may be comprehended, without the trouble of interpretation. Every one knows the feasts of Harvest Home, the various scenes of a fair, a race-ground, &c. We might equally represent in pantomime such subjects as, like tragedy and comedy, have an intrigue and a *denouement*, and, for the intelligence of the spectator, it will suffice to express the sentiments of the personages with exactitude.

Let us suppose a shepherd suddenly inflamed at the sight of a young and beautiful shepherdess. He approaches her with a tender respect ; timid modesty engages the damsel to avoid this new lover ; she quits the scene ; after a short absence she reappears, apparently confused, but secretly charmed at reviewing him : he comprehends this prompt return, and, sensible of the favour, lays a riband or a nosegay at the feet of the shepherdess. His happiness is yet uncertain, whilst a second lover surprises them ; a scene of jealousy commences, but the conduct of the shepherdess proves that she has not given the intruder any power over her heart. The shepherdess, who has more ancient claims on the heart of the second lover, now arrives : her pride, her choler, her sadness, her dejection urge the faithless swain to resume his former fetters, and his confusion and penitence, joined to the good offices of the first couple, obtain his pardon, after which, penetrated with gratitude, he in turn labours for the felicity of his benefactor. When the action commences, proceeds, and terminates in this manner, what obscurity or what ambiguity can any of these situations offer to the minds of the spectators? The play of the motions and attitudes of the personages, the sentiments so naturally adapted to the man, suffice to define themselves, and no one will demand the explanation of a *denouement*, of which every romance and the daily events of life offer at once the example and the interpretation. Here the eye makes the exposition of the subject, and the heart explains the recital.

Notwithstanding this pantomime is not essentially confined to ordinary and daily events, Father Lafiteau says, in his work entitled " The Manners of the Savages,"—" Many of those who have lived amongst the Iroquois have assured me, that often, after a chief of war, on his return, represents all which had passed in his expedition, and in the assault she had made on or sustained from his enemies, without the omission of any circumstance, then all those who are present at this recital rise to dance, and represent these actions with as much vivacity as if they had actually assisted at them, without having been prepared for such a feat or even concerting it among themselves."

You here see it is not necessary that the events should be of those kinds which happen ordinarily in war; they may be attended by

what circumstances you will, provided they be
accompanied and indicated by attitudes and gestures most true and most expressive. Then
each who, attentive to the recital of these
events, shall have impressed the circumstances
as they follow each other in his memory, will
also comprehend the dance, from its beginning
to the end, and at each new scene he will be
able to indicate the recital which he ought to
represent.

The same thing occurs in the pantomime subjects which are executed upon our modern theatres. Although it be not a common event or
daily occurrence which is represented, it will suffice to know the kind, the cause, the progression,
and the developement : it will be necessary to recognise the name of the pantomime, or to cast
a *coup d'œil* over the *program,* and then there
will not be any difficulty in following the attitudes and motions of the dancers, and thoroughly
making out their meaning.

Often even we shall have no need of either
name or program ; for the groups of personages,
or, perhaps, such or such a circumstance, proper
to the determinate action, are able to indicate,
on the spot, the event which is about to be represented.

Thus it was on the ancient theatres, during the representation of the Royal Shepherd of Mount Ida. It was sufficient to recognise the three Goddesses, and the traits which distinguished the one from the other; it was only necessary to see the shepherd on the mountain, or, more especially, the golden apple which had inflamed the jealousy of the three rivals, and every body was well aware of all that was to ensue. Nothing would then be either equivocal or unintelligible, either in the countenances and movements of Juno, of Minerva, or of Venus, or in the different expressions of Paris, who at first is struck with admiration, afterwards with indecision, and lastly subjugated by the conquering charms of the Queen of Beauty. The same thing would take place on our own theatres, if it were permitted to convert the stories from the sacred history into ballets of action. All the world is acquainted with them, and he who should see a man and a woman under a tree, with a serpent twisting round the trunk, would, without the least difficulty, comprehend the meaning of all the rest ; even to the cherubim armed with the flaming sword. Clarke, without understanding Spanish, perfectly comprehended the whole mystery of the Passion, as represented at Madrid.—*(See Letters concerning the Spanish Nation, by the Reverend Edward Clarke.)*

A very slight examination will convince you, that such subjects as I have just been pointing out to you by no means oblige pantomime to dispense with the rule established for the comedian.

Where the design to animate the idea of certain objects, even to the highest pitch of intuition, predominates in pantomime (a condition which also admits the most complete latitude to the actor) or where the whole subject is perfectly intelligible by the simple expression of the sentiments, or where it is known beforehand by its intrigue and by its progress of action, then the sole contemplation and the series of developed sentiments form the recital, or, rather, they appear to form it; for, in the end, it is the spectator who creates it for himself.

If, in all these cases, pantomime stands in need of but little assistance to render itself intelligible to the spectator, why should it not rather attach itself to giving the most strong and animated expressions to the sentiments with which the soul is penetrated? Why should it

seek to express what it can never render intelligible, or only mark in a very imperfect way;
and in making useless efforts to this effect, in
sacrificing, entirely neglecting, or weakening the
expression of the affections of the soul, which it
could nevertheless render so easily.

In comparing the subjects of the ancient pantomimes among themselves, of which some notions have come down to us, and particularly in
reading the long list which Lucian has given us
of them, I find that this art never employed itself
in the invention of the subject, which was always
founded on some fable, on mythology, or on
events in the history of former times, and which
were grown familiar by tradition.   This circumstance renders all the marvellous things related
of Pylades, Bathyllus, and other pantomimes
posterior to them, easy to be conceived; whilst,
without this circumstance, simple as it may appear, it would be almost impossible to form any
idea of them.

The spectators, at least the greater part of
them, knew beforehand all those celebrated pantomimes wished to indicate and express; and
the force of the voluntary illusion easily led
them to the false consequence, that the sole

play of looks and gestures communicated to
them all the ideas; whilst these ideas, a long
time lulled asleep in the memory, stood in need
of only a slight impulsion to rouse and to awaken
them.

It is thus necessary, I think, to explain the
exclamation of the Cynic Demetrius, related by
Lucian *, and the anecdote of the Royal Prince
of Pontus, who besought Nero to make him a
present of a pantomime, that he might be able
to dispense with an interpreter, and employ *him*
in all his negociations with the Barbarians. Supposing that the pantomime at which this prince
was present was not founded on one of those
common actions, of which the ordinary feelings
of human life and daily occurrences were able
to indicate the sense or facilitate the knowledge; if this were the case, I say, I do not see
any other method of explaining this anecdote
without involving myself in infinite difficulty
and perplexity. The most perfect play of *gesture* could not any how instruct this prince in
an action of which he had no previous know-

* Ακѕω, ανθρωπε, ὰ ποιεις, ουχ᾽ ὁρω μονον αλλα μοι δοκεις
Ταις χερσιν αυταις λαλειν.

ledge.   The most that this play could have done was to have conducted him to form *guesses* on the subject of the scene, but it could never have indicated it to him with clearness and precision.

If the play of pantomime was a sort of language, then another difficulty would present itself; for one cannot conceive how the language could be intelligible to a foreign Prince who had never studied its elements.   Certainly a similar language could not subsist in an assemblage of arbitrary and accidental signs, of which no exterior objects presented either motive or modification; for no language ever was, or ever will be, formed in this manner.   Notwithstanding this, pantomimical language will partake the inconvenience of all other languages, of being forced to recur to certain radical signs, and to analogies which, in designing equally a crowd of objects, do not indicate any with exactitude and precision, and of which it is impossible to divine the true signification, without first having gained a ground work by instruction or by practice.   The language which *Rabelais* makes *Panurge* speak might be composed of signs well chosen and aptly adapted, without its

being at all less an unintelligible GALIMATHIAS
for me, even when the expressions and the turns
of the ancient French dialect are familiar to
me.

Œuvres de Rabelais, T. 1, ch. 16. " Comment
Panurge fit quinault l'Anglois qui arguoit par
signes." Saint Augustin has said nearly the
same thing, in proving, by the example of the
Carthaginians, how difficult it is to comprehend
a language made up of signs, of which the elements have not been studied.

" *Quia multis modis simile aliquid alicui potest*
esse, non constant talia signa inter homines nisi
consensus accedat."—*De Doct. Christ.*

He reports that, during the establishment of
pantomime at Carthage, an interpreter was necessary to explain them to the people. It remains to know, if the real object of this explanation was not to instruct the public in subjects
selected from fable or history, and represented
on the scene, as well as to render the signs and
attitudes of the dancers intelligible by a knowledge of their subjects, and thus to illustrate the
first by the means of the second: for I cannot

form to myself any idea of an assemblage of signs, such as the ancient pantomime ought to have been, and the richness of which would have equaled the most complete collection of signs, general and particular, which compose our modern languages, and could express and communicate new thoughts by a perpetual variety in its combinations.

Certainly a similar language could not be either created or understood with great facility.

LETTER XXVII.

Mr. Noverre's Idea of a Pantomime—The Ballet founded on the celebrated Story of the Horatii and the Curiatii— Example of the Outre in Pantomime.

THE pantomime of modern times has no advantage over that of ancient date; for, whilst renouncing known and common actions, it pretends to the executing subjects mixed with intrigue, and, of its own invention, it finds itself in an alternative either of painting in signs as expressive as it can possibly create, of leaving to a hazard that which their vague and uncertain signification will allow the spectators to lay hold of, or appealing to the aid of the interpreter to explain, by *word*, that which the look, attitude, and gesture are inadequate to express. Mr. Noverre absolutely rejects this last expedient. According to him, the art which has recourse to such methods is only in its infancy, and can merely stammer.

" Sous le règne de Louis XIV. les récits, les

dialogues, et les monologues servoient d'inter-
prètes à la danse. Elle ne faisoit que bégayer,
ses sons foibles et inarticules avoient besoin d'être
soutenus par la musique, et d'être expliqués
par la poësie.—*Lettres sur la Danse et sur les
Ballets.*

This author declares himself equally against
the use of picturesque and uncertain signs : for,
though he does not treat the subject *formally,*
we may, nevertheless (as far as I can recollect),
draw this consequence from the rest of his
system.

First, he avows, " that modern pantomime is
more cramped than it was in the days of Augustus." I reply to this, that it can only be attributed to the vast and probably exaggerated
ideas we entertain from perusing the swelled-up
praises of the ancients. " There are a quantity
of things," continues he, " which can only render themselves intelligible by the aid of gestures :
nothing of the species of tranquil dialogue ought
to find place in a pantomime."

In another passage, where he criticises the aid
of words for the explanation of a ballet, and compares those which have need of this assistance to
the pictures of those painters who, in the infancy

of the art, made use of large rolls of paper, which, coming out of the mouths of the figures, explained their actions, motives, &c. &c. &c. he thus expresses himself in his ingenious work.

" Lorsque les danseurs animés par le sentiment se transformeront sous mille formes différentes avec les traits variés des passions; lorsqu'ils seront des Protées, et que leur physionomie, leurs égards traceront tous les mouvemens de leur áme; lorsque leurs bras sortiront de ce chemin étroit que l'école leur a prescrit, et que, parcourant avec autant de grace que de vérité un espace plus considérable, ils décriront par des positions justes les mouvemens successifs des passions; lorsqu'enfin ils associeront l'esprit et le génie à leur art, ils se distingueront; les *récits* dès lors deviendront *inutiles*, tout parlera, chaque mouvement sera expressif, chaque attitude peindra une situation, chaque geste dévoilera une intention, chaque regard annoncera un nouveau sentiment, tout sera séduisant, parce que tout sera vrai, et que l'imitation sera prise dans la nature."

According to my judgment, it clearly results from these passages (a multiplicity of which I

could quote if necessary) that the first master of
this art, and the best author who ever treated it,
banishes from his theatre every thing which is not
intelligible by the expression of the sentiment.
But *what* subjects will he discuss, if he rejects
common actions and daily occurrences? The
ancient pantomimes were allowed the permission
of taking their subjects from sacred history; an
advantage which ours do not enjoy—for similar
exhibitions equally displease the incredulous and
devotee, though, perhaps, the latter in a lesser
degree than the former. Then there only remains the second mode employed by the ancients; I mean to say, to put into scenic action
the best known works of the poets, and to bring
them to the memory of the spectator as well as
they are able. Thus the opinions and proceed-
ings of all those who have sought to carry modern
pantomime to the perfection of the ancient perfectly accords with what I have just said upon the
subject.

Abbé Du Bos, from whom it is useless to
quote the passage by which he proves the necessity of selecting well known subjects for pantomime, recounts the first essay made at Paris for
the restoration of this art, in imitation of the ancients.

" A princess," says he, " who joined much
acquired knowledge to a natural quickness, and
who had a great taste for dramatic exhibitions,
wished to see an essay of the art of ancient pantomimes, which might give her more certain ideas
of their representation than those she had conceived in reading such authors as had written on
the subject.   For want of actors versed in the
art of which we have been speaking, she selected
a male and female dancer, who were both of superior merit in their profession, and gifted with a
talent for invention.   They had a subject given
them to be represented by gesture : it was the
scene in Corneille's tragedy, where the young
Horatius kills his sister.   This they executed to
the sound of several instruments, which played
music composed expressly for this scene by a
skilful artist.   Our two new pantomime novi-
ciates animated each other, by their gestures,
with such reciprocal skill that they burst into
tears themselves : it would be superfluous to add,
that the spectators were equally affected."

M. Noverre has completed this rude essay,
made with one scene only, in putting the whole
play into a ballet of action, and has thought
proper to do the same thing with several other

dramas; but he requires that they should be known by the spectators, because, without this essential precaution, the pantomime could never be intelligible. " The pieces," says he, " in which Pylades and Bathyllus performed were well known; they served as programs to the spectators, who having engraved them in their memories followed the actor without labour, and anticipated every coming expression. Shall we not then have the same advantages when we put the most favourite dramas of our own theatre into action? Is our organization less perfect than that of the dancers of Rome? and may not all that was done in the days of Augustus be as well done now? To doubt it would be to lessen mankind—to libel the age in which we live.

I have wished to prove, by the sentiment and by the method practised by the best known author of this art, what in effect results from the nature of the thing, to wit, that it is needful to guard against unknown subjects; for that which is unintelligible can neither please nor affect nor produce any lasting emotion in the soul. The imposing magic of groupes gracefully disposed, the taste, riches, and magnificence of the decorations, combined with the accompaniments of harmonious music—all these things, I say, may flat-

ter and amuse the spectator, but it is absolutely
impossible that the subject itself, as a dramatic
action, and a developement of situations and
events, can *interest*. The charm resulting from
it will be only for the *eyes ;* the spirit will there
find no enjoyment, and the heart will still continue void and vacant. The rule of expression,
established for the actor, remains then in full
force for pantomime. When subjects already
known are treated, every thing depends on the
order and progression of the pantomime ; for if,
in the execution of each particular scene, the advice of M. Noverre, with respect to the general
plan, is not observed, if the events are not connected, if, neglecting to concentrate the scattered tableaux, the action is rendered slow and
dragging, if, servilely marching in the trammels
of the poet through the whole progression of his
ideas, each gesture, each attitude, each expression is given servilely by gestures, every advantage gained on one side will be lost on the
other. The play of pantomime will then become
fatiguing, and unintelligible in many of its parts ;
for where is the spectator who can recall every
expression which the poet made use of? This
play will consist in repetitions of monotonous expressions, or, at least, very similar one to the

other; or it will wander into caricatures, insufficient, extraordinary, perhaps misplaced, and almost constantly prejudicial to the expression, if they do not destroy it entirely. I say misplaced, because an image, which may be noble, grand, or terrible to the imagination, rendered in pantomime, will frequently if not always become low, trivial, and grotesque.

I do not know if you have ever been present at the representation of M. Noverre's ballet of the Horatii, of which a very bad sample was given once or twice. What a galimatias was assembled together, to express the passage where Camilla (in our English tragedy of the Roman Father, this lady is called Horatia) curses her brother, her country, and all the Roman citizens. Nothing could be more despicable than the way of representing these verses—

Qu'elle-même (Rome) sur soi renverse ses *murailles*,
Et de ses propres mains déchire ses entrailles!
Les Horaces, Acte iv.

This idea is not only noble and grand of itself but at the same time terrible for the imagination. We think we behold an immense and profound gulf open, like the jaws of some terrible monster, to consume and destroy the whole of a vast and puissant people. But how ridiculously and contemptibly low would this appear, if represented in pantomime; and, likewise, how disgusting would it appear in representation. Suppose a dancer pointing to the bottom of the scene (apparently to indicate the spot where we are to imagine the city of Rome); subsequently agitating her hand, directed downwards to the earth; afterwards suddenly opening, not the jaws of a monster, but her own little mouth, and thither conveying her clenched fist, from time to time, as if she meant to swallow it with the greatest avidity. *(See Plate* XXXIV.)

The major part of the spectators would burst into loud fits of laughter, whilst the remaining portion would find themselves at a loss to conceive the meaning of this unexpected action; for, in effect, the explication I have been giving of this farce is not conjectural, and it is easily possible to furnish another of a nature totally different. If one ever could invent a language of gesture, which really deserved that name, these servile imitations of language, as it is spoken, would be regarded as miserable translations, in which the style of the original would be sought in vain.

LETTER XXVIII.

Farther Disquisition on the Subject of Pantomime.

Iꜰ pantomime, elevating itself above such events as are taken from the ordinary and daily occurrences of life, is forced to treat of subjects anterior and well known, the most complete proof of the impuissance and dependance of its art will result from it ; viz. that it appears not to have any need of the assistance of words, and yet to be incapable of proceeding *without them*.   Moreover, the details of each scene, in particular of the tragic and comic chef d'œuvres, not being perfectly known by all the beholders, the play of the pantomime will remain an enigma in several of its parts, to the greater number of such spectators: so that many of the links in the connecting chain will be entirely broken : in short, if all tranquil dialogue ought to be suppressed to accelerate the action, then pantomime will sacrifice precisely what most charms the enlightened connoisseur in theatrical representation, to wit, the *complete image* of characters, with their just *mélange*, and in the reciprocal proportion of the affections and faculties of the soul, the complete developement of the play of the passions (of which the shades are frequently so fine), as well as their motives and most secret resources.

In spite of all these inconveniences, panto-mime can still have its charms.   The senses may be enriched, where the understanding is lost; and it was not, certainly, the soul which was much a gainer amongst the Romans who, you say, were so passionately fond of this kind of spectacle.

But would it not be possible, you add, to re-gain what has been lost of this art?—to create, in time, what has perhaps never yet existed? Why should a language, formed of mien, ges-tures, and attitudes, be a thing less possible than a language formed out of articulate sounds?

Supposing, my friend, that this might be pro-bable, it must, nevertheless, be confessed that, in our days, the conditions which might favour the discovery of a similar language of pantomime do not exist.   Each idiom, for as much as I know, owes its origin to a very small society of men : the perfection costs incredible efforts of genius. Necessity, the father of all discoveries, creates

and achieves it. But *now*, that all large societies are *already* established, genius, whatever may
be its boldness and temerity, will ever be alarmed
at the impossibility of equaling oral language by
that of pantomime, and will consequently renounce the undertaking.

The necessity of a mute language no longer
exists, because the different idioms, now come to
perfection in the world, suffice for all occasions
where men are desirous of communicating their
sentiments or their ideas. The existence of a
language of pantomime, which could come in
comparison with one of speech, is hardly possible; for although mankind is liable to run into a
thousand follies and extravagances, it is hardly
credible that a nation, accustomed to a verbal
language (as all the known people in the world
are), should addict itself for ages to the acquisition of a thing totally *useless*, the necessity of
which could not be demonstrated by any possible
cause. Moreover I am doubtful whether the existence of *verbal* language would be able to facilitate the discovery of a *pantomimical* one; on
the contrary, greater difficulty would arise from
it; for it is very probable that we should seek to
create this language after the model of existing
idioms; and it would be still a material question

to know, if the natural forms of the one would be also those of the other.   But I ought here to retract what I have granted to you before, *i. e.* that the invention of a pantomimical language is as possible and as easy as the discovery of an oral one.   As for the different advantages that the signs which strike the ear have over those which affect the organ of sight, I shall confine myself to a slight and rapid observation.

Man, in the employment of words, has a double intention : he wishes to communicate the ideas of those objects which affect him, and he seeks to indicate the manner in which he is affected by them.   If even he should not have this latter intention, it would not be the less an interior and imperious need of his nature, which, in a state of passion, he could not prevent himself from satisfying.   To this effect oral language has its interjections, and pantomime its gestures of expression.—These, when even they have not so much force and vivacity as the former, are nevertheless more clear, more varied, and perhaps more determined, and the will is less in a state to master them than articulated sounds.

The tones by which man imitates all that strikes on the organ of hearing were, in verbal language, the first elements he could employ to mark the objects of his thoughts. It would then be necessary, in the language of pantomime, that the imitation of visible objects should take place of these elements; since, as I have already said, signs purely arbitrary, and deprived of every kind of motive, cannot become the basis of any language whatsoever: these primitive signs ought afterwards to serve as a type to all those that, conformably to the figures and varied turns of a language it would be necessary to create, indicate the remainder of our other ideas: and why would it not be as possible to arrive at this by the means of looks and gestures as by the aid of sounds? Why could not visible images also designate the various connections and abstractions which the mind, the judgment, and the imagination execute relatively to the ideas? Hitherto, the language of pantomime appears nearly as practicable as *verbal language:* notwithstanding, a circumstance of some importance remains to be examined.

In a language spoken, the interjection or the expression of the sentiment is never but a sound —an expiration; but in pantomime it is a complete, proper, finished attitude. In the first, the imitative sound, which contains the idea of the object, is able to unite itself very intimately with the tone or expiration, which satisfies the sentiment. In the second case, the reunion of the painting and the expression is impossible, where the one and the other ought to operate by the same parts of the body, whilst each demands a totally different employment of it.

The word love is, without contradiction, impressive, as well as the action or attitude made use of to express this affection, it paints the languor, softness, and charm of this sentiment; nevertheless, this word once found, you can pronounce it, not only with a soft and tender inflexion, but also with an accent plaintive, sad, choleric, furious, bitter, or sarcastical, without one title of this word's becoming confused, and, consequently without the idea of the object losing any of its perspicuity.—Here all depends solely on the modification of such or such an organ or expiration, which renders the tone of the voice low or elevated, soft or rough, flat or sharp, trembling or decided.

On the other hand, endeavour to reunite to the picturesque gesture of love, varied pantomimical expressions, and such as are connected in a very intimate manner, without the gesture finding itself destroyed, or becoming less obscure, difficult, and equivocal; then you will perceive

the impossibility, or at least the extreme difficulty of this reunion. Sometimes one contradiction will impede this mixture. The eye languishing and dying, the attitude bending with grace,
or softly indolent with love (as when Felix leans
over the chair of his weeping Violante *(Plate*
XXXV.) cannot, by any means accord with the
sparkling, undecided look, with the muscles extended and indicative of choler, as when the fiery
young Spaniard is accusing her of perfidy and
falsehood. *(See Plate* XXXVI.) These gestures
accord as little as the cringing, humiliated air of
a flatterer, who, with curved body and sinking
knee, takes by turn the honied and respectful tone,
(as in Plate XXXVII.) can assimilate to the
proud Hamlet, who neither hides his contempt
nor his indignation. *(See Plate* XXXVIII.)

Sometimes, whilst this reunion is not of itself
impossible, we shall be uncertain if in the play of
gestures, the looks or the attitude ought, in their
ensemble, to express or designate a mixed sentiment.

When I see a soft smile wandering round the
mouth and cheeks of a person, whilst the interior
angles of his eyebrows are elevated, how is it possible for me to answer the question, whether the
two sentiments, *i. e.* love and sorrow, reunite

themselves in the soul of him who presents this attitude, or if only the first of these sentiments affects his soul, whilst the second is simply the object which produces the first, and so *vice versa;* and, in the last case, how shall I be able to decide which of these two sentiments is typical, or which is imitative? Since these two things are equally possible: love can excite sadness—sadness love.

I am not ignorant that in this case the connexion and series of ideas are capable of affording much eclaircissement. Nevertheless one should not require too much, for in doing so we run the risk of not gaining *any* intelligence concerning the subject which we are investigating.

LETTER XXIX.

More Remarks on the ancient Pantomime Dancers—The Art of Gesture considered musically—Remark to prove that all musical Arts are founded on the same Rules and Principles.

THE rapid reflections with which I finished my last letter, and the fear, either of being prolix, or falling into minute subtilties, prevent me from much amplification. The discovery of a panto-mimical language, I have urged, if not proved, is a very difficult problem to resolve. Notwith-standing all that has been said concerning the age of Augustus, I find it impossible to join in opinion with those moderns who exalt the mar-vellous effects of dancing among the ancients to the skies. According to the testimony of au-thors, the pantomimes of antiquity certainly had some particular signs. I will even grant more than this, that they possessed farther than what solely appertained to their art, which they made it a particular, and, probably, a unique study, during the whole course of their lives, to raise, on all occasions, the most expressive and most characteristical traits, that oral language furnished them with a number of happy images and allusions; that they executed all these signs with a truth and energy of which we have a difficulty of forming any conception in our cold climates; that they carried expression to its highest pitch, and seized hold of its finest traits. But, allowing them all these advantages, at what an immense distance must they yet have been from oral language. A Pylades and a Bathyllus surely had not in themselves more knowledge than all the rest of mankind put together.

By a general and marvellous impulsion, the whole Roman people would not have applied to a new language, useless to every other need and occasion. After this reasoning, I cannot form any idea to myself of the execution of an intelligible pantomime, intelligible in its own proper resources, or scenes of a tranquil discussion, and of the developement of an intrigue, carried on with art and address, without the aid of words. The collection of the signs of these pantomime dancers, perhaps, was no more than in our own days we should expect from the dictionary of a people whose minds were hardly emerged from barbarism. Common and material ideas will suffice for a narrow circle ; but it will be too poor, in calculative and abstracted ideas, for a play, or even a scene of Euripides, to have been trans-lated into a similar language.

I hope you will not here oppose to me the pantomime language of the Sicilians, of which M. Le Comte de Borch speaks with such rap-tures in his Letters upon Sicily and the Isle of Malta, *Tom.* 2. *Letter* 20. *p. 36.*

"Another particularity, not less singular (the characteristical properties of the Sicilian lan-guage had been the argument), is the usage of gestures and signs commonly employed here, and of which the language is so expressive for the natives that at a considerable distance, in the midst of a numerous company, two persons, without opening the mouth, mutually compre-hend and communicate their thoughts one to the other : these signs and these gestures are by no means general. A woman has several different kinds of them ; one sort for her husband, another for her lover, and a third for her friends. This difference of alphabet produces three distinct lan-guages, of which the same person makes use with all possible facility. The same skill is re-markable amongst the children, who, from the most tender age, commence composing, with their playmates, a set of signs proper to themselves alone : this arises from the *penchant* of the nation for gestures. A Sicilian cannot speak the most indifferent word, without following it up with an expressive gesture ; it is thought that these signs and gestures take their date from Denis the Ancient, whose tyranny forbidding the use of words to his subjects, obliged them to invent new modes of communicating their thoughts, and consoling each other in their state of sorrow. I will not guarantee the truth of this origin, but from whatever source the custom comes, I cannot help admiring it, and telling you that I consider it the most sublime pantomime I ever witnessed in the course of my life."

Pay attention, if you please, to the essential circumstances contained in the narrative of this traveller. Each person has his particular language, which he knows how to vary according to the interlocutors. There is a multitude, then, of languages of this kind, of which each is original, and invented by the person who makes use of it ; from these facts, of which the certainty cannot be contested, ought we not to conclude that the Sicilians have but a small number of signs to manifest their ideas, and that the employment of such signs is circumscribed in a very narrow circle ? But (you may yet object to me), since the signs of pantomimes render their subjects so little intelligible, and that, during the representations, all depended upon a preliminary knowledge of the event brought forward on the scene, and on the retentive memory of the spectators, what was the use of these signs ? Why did the pantomimes obstinately retain what they might have so easily done without ? Perhaps it was because they did not perceive the inutility of it, or that a self-vanity did not permit them to avow the deficiency and inefficacy of their art, either to themselves or to their spectators.

On the subject of these pantomimes the ancient authors have only left us a paucity of notions; and it clearly appears that they have been noticed by them in a manner too concise, too vague, and too hyperbolical.

Enough, my friend, upon a subject almost inexhaustible, and on which I should have said less, had not your questions and objections obliged me to be diffuse. Let us now no longer speak of the art of gesture and theatrical action, as it belongs to painting, and serves to represent the single moment of an action : let us occupy ourselves with this art, as it produces its effects successively. In one word, let us consider it as *music*. You

see I here use the word music in the acceptation
as taken by the ancient Greeks, in the most general and extensive sense, as containing many
other arts, united since their origin, and which
have only been subsequently separated.

I know not whether this abstraction has been
most useful or prejudicial to them. These arts
comprehended in the word *music* were for the
eye,—the art of gesture, the movements of the
body, with their lyrical part—to wit, dancing :
for the organ of hearing, the arts of declamation,
with *its* lyrical part also, which comprehended
singing and the accompaniment of music and its
instruments.

Poetry, considered relatively to the mechanism of the verses and the selection of rhythm by
which it delights a delicate ear, also belonging to
it. I flatter myself that you will dispense with my
proving, that neither the arts I have here been
enumerating nor any other have been really de-
signed by the word music : you may convince
yourself of this by the passages which Brown
and Du Bos have extracted on this subject from
Plato, St. Augustin, Quintilian, &c.—*(Considerations on Poetry and Music, Section 5.)*

In comparing the fine arts, of which I have
been speaking, one with the other, you will soon

perceive that the ancient idea of music reunited
the two essential characters, to wit—the *energetic,* or that which only acted successively by
degrees; and the *sensible,* or that which struck
instantaneously upon the senses.   The one ex-
cluded from it all the arts of imitation which
immediately act upon the senses, and the other
dispensed with poetry, inasmuch as it speaks not
only to the senses, but to the imagination, and
to the other faculties of the soul.   You can, in
truth, object to me against this last character,
that Socrates, in Plato, not only calls philosophy
music, but *music by excellence ;* notwithstanding
this science, which uniquely occupies the judgment and the mind, has nothing in common with
the senses.   But if philosophy has been, in effect,
regarded as forming one of the parts of music,
wherefore did Socrates, at the approach of death,
occupy himself with doubt, if, in studying this
science, he had obeyed the Divinity who ordered
him to study music ? Why, in supposing that the
Divinity had prescribed the study of music, taken
in the ordinary sense, (δηκωδη μϩσικην) did he yet
make verses in his prison ?

Every man familiar with the works of Plato has
remarked it as an essential character of his manner of writing, that he always pleases himself in

connecting the arts with serious and scientific subjects, and that he willingly borrows the charms of the beautiful for the sciences; and, on the other hand, the aid of the severity and dignity of science, for the beautiful. In like manner as he here calls philosophy music by excellence, he elsewhere denominates a complete government— the most perfect tragedy.—*De Legib. lib. 7.*

He here considers the statesman as the colleague and fellow-labourer of the tragic poet. Would you, for this reason, reckon the ancient governments among the pieces of the theatre, and place the great statesmen of antiquity, such as Solon, Pericles, or Lycurgus, in the list of tragic poets? It appears, from a passage of the Phedon, that not poetry in general, but solely the mechanical art of versification was comprised in music : for how could Socrates imagine himself fulfilling the order he had received in a dream, by simply putting the Fables of Æsop into verse, which, existing from a long time, were also well known to all Greece?

I beseech you, my dear friend, not to consider it as an absolutely useless digression, if, in the transition from one branch of the art of gesture and theatrical action to the other, I speak of the idea which the ancients entertained of music. I foresee that, in the number of researches we have yet to make, it will be very advantageous to generalize our reflections, and to transport them from the too circumscribed field of this art into the more extended *plain* of *music*.

Browne regrets the separation of the different energetic arts in their exercise : for my own part, I do not less regret their separation from that general idea which embraced them all.

If the first of these abstractions has injured the effects of these arts, their theory has lost infinitely by the second. What is to follow will prove, I trust, that all the arts are really founded on the same general ideas, and that they have all the same rule. You may already perceive the truth of this principle, if you wish to apply the principles of the arts of gesture and theatrical action to the art of declamation, which is intimately combined and connected with it. I call those *energetic* arts, which act successively and by degrees upon the soul, such as song, declamation, pantomime, &c. and I give the name of *sensible arts* to those of which the effects are made perceptible on the spot, as painting, sculpture, &c.

You are right when you observe, that, to be in a proper state to appreciate the resemblance which exists between the fundamental ideas of the art of gesture and that of declamation, it would at least be necessary to have a sample of the latter. But would you be really puzzled to attain this? Do you not know any of those numerous works composed by authors ancient and modern upon this theory? Can I presume that you are ignorant of the existence of a Cicero, a Quintilian, and, above all, the famous Stagirite, whose works were the guide of these two celebrated Romans?

In truth, the latter, according to his common custom, passes very lightly over this matter; instead of the theory itself, he only scatters the germ, of which the developement may afford all we seek: each future plant is contained in its organized seed; and if this great man does not himself develope the matter we are here speaking upon, the too great richness of his fancy is undoubtedly the cause. Like parent Nature, who, in the immensity of the different modifications of matter, can neither follow all her productions, nor bring them to equal perfection— so this great man has not been able to adhere to each idea which his sublime and fertile mind had suggested to him.

Aristotle says, that many authors, and among others, Glaucos of Teos, in Ionia, have shown how pieces of poetry ought to be declaimed, but that no one had mentioned the art of oratorical declamation.

" This last art," continues he, " depends upon the voice, for the knowledge of each expression of particular passion : for example—when it is necessary to raise or to sink it, or to speak in the ordinary tone. The same thing holds good with respect to the different tones, which are the sharp, the grave, and the middle; and equally with respect to the number, to the end that they may be well directed in each particular movement *."

I presume that the mode of rendering this passage of Aristotle, in translating it, and commenting on it at the same time, will not displease you. I wish to leave you to judge, if there would not be a method of bringing back to the three points indicated by this philosopher, that which Cicero calls " Plura ab his delapsa genera—the

* Ετι δε αυτη μεν (ἡ ὑποκρισις) εν τη φονη, πως αυτη δεί χρησθαι προς ἑκαστον παθος οίον ποτε μεγαλη, καὶ ποτε μίκρα, καὶ ποτε μεση. Καὶ τοις τονοις οιον οξεια καὶ βαρεια καὶ μεση, καὶ ρυθμοις τισι προς ἑκατα. Τρια γαρ ετι περι ὧν σκοπυσι ταυτα δ'εστι μεγεθος, αρμ-νια ρυθμος.—Rhetor. l. 3. Edit. Leps. p. 182.

læve, asperum," &c. In the explication of the second point, I discard, in truth, the opinion of the commentators, and, I believe, with reason; since it is impossible that the argument here can be the manner of accenting the syllables solely. The philosopher does not speak of the art of good reading, but of that of good declamation, with the expression suitable to each passion; and although this last talent always presupposes the former, the one may nevertheless exist without the other. There are many orators and actors who are scarcely deficient as to the proper accents of words and syllables, but very often in that which suits the actual passion of the soul. In the mean time place the veritable method of declamation (it imports not what passion it is needful to express) under the three points of view established by Aristotle; and, in developing the motives which modify the shades of the accent of each passion; in rendering this accent sharp or grave, rapid or slow, sonorous or deaf, &c. you will always fall, as in the art of gesture, upon the analogy, upon the intention or the design, and upon the change of the state of the body. The slow progression of the ideas, which in admiration stops itself at each circumstance, and renders the attitude and gesture proper to this affection so solemn, impresses the same shades to each tone, in making similar words and syllables follow and connect with each other.

In joy the progression of ideas is quick and animated, but always light and soft; and, conformably to this analogy, while joy breaks out in words, while its language is full of mirth and grace, choler has a short respiration, on account of the interior trouble it excites. The savage and untameable character of this passion betrays itself even by stammering when it acquires vivacity, and by an absolute silence when it is arrived at its highest pitch.

In the first case, the soul, launched out with too much vehemence, can no longer return back, to supply all which is intermediate between the expressed idea and that which already has offered itself to the thought. In the other, the soul entirely despairs of transforming the abundance of its ideas into words, or to be able to follow their unmeasured celerity with the voice. The analogy of the succession of the ideas serves likewise to afford reason for the choice of particular sounds. —You will find that in admiration the tone is never sharp, but always grave—why?—because it only developes its ideas very slowly. You will smile at this idea ; but try if, in generalizing it, you may not apply it to all the passions.

Choler, which in speech rolls like an impetuous torrent, often bewilders itself in sharp and whistling tones, and takes the highest notes precisely when fury renders it most dangerous or most disposed to an attack ; and when it seeks to humiliate an adversary by contempt—how many times does the voice fail in the midst of those cries which ought to be uttered with the greatest vehemence ?

On the contrary, the smile of a soft joy will be light, agreeable, and brilliant. This affection constantly modulates between sharp and shrill tones, because the march of ideas is rapid and animated, but not savage and impetuous. It has the power of elevating and depressing the tone according to the different degrees of its vivacity, without ever giving into the piercing shriekings of choler nor into the grave and solemn intonations of admiration. Equally distant from the two extremes, the voice always balances itself in the medium of its force : and this is precisely the reason why the expression of no other passion is so sonorous, so agreeable, so full of grace, for the middle and moderate tones have more of beauty and concord; although the bad taste of our modern connoisseurs and virtuosos, who use every effort to do away this impression, tends to prove to the contrary.

To these remarks, others might be subjoined, which are intimately connected with them, and which concern certain modifications of the voice, purposely made, whether we wish to afford assistance to the mind, or whether the intention be to smother, excite, or moderate the affections. He who mutters to himself, or recites to others an important and difficult thought, will carefully and more precisely examine and appreciate it; he will give it, not only a slow and distinct phraseology, but he will also make use of a more grave tone; because, accordingly, to the manner in which he is affected, a similar intonation awakens and fixes the attention, and disposes the soul to that calm tranquillity, to that moderate progression of ideas, which so well second *research* and the most perfect ascertainment of *truth*. Another, which accumulates ideas to aggrandize the sentiment of respect and dispose the soul to adore the object of its veneration with more fervour and humility, will lower the tone at each word; whilst that which wishes to reinforce the affections (such, for example, as terror, joy, or choler) will successively elevate the voice. I must here just remark, that the passions, in general, have each their proper gradation, which does not simply consist in elevating or reinforcing the voice, but in the *roundness*, the most perfect manner of rendering the particular tone which appertains to each. He who proposes to appease a man inflamed with choler, that is to say, to alter the rough and impetuous march of his ideas to a more slow and moderate progression, will guard against taking too elevated a tone, or speaking with too much vivacity, or in a boisterous way; for if he should so act, whatever might be the nature of his remonstrances, far from producing the least effect, the disagreeable impressions which would result from it on the organs of the choleric man would tend more to accelerate than to moderate the march of his ideas, or give them a different direction. The well known pitchpipe of C. Gracchus, perhaps, less indicated the proper intonation for the moment than it guaranteed him from extremes: it moderated the fire of the orator by its grave sounds, and by its sharp notes it roused him when he grew flat and vapid.

By examples, taken from many passions, it would be very easy to prove to you the fecundity of the principle of analogy. It would not be less easy to convince you, that, at each small modification of an affection, as at each admixture of one affection with another, the tone of the voice likewise experiences a change : for example, that veneration, when it ceases to be a pure admiration of moral perfections, and is mingled with fear and shame, loses the gravity, roundness, and equality of tone, that the respiration instantly becomes difficult, and that the phrases are consequently shorter and less connected, &c. But I shall confine myself to the indication of the rout which you may be able to follow in your own proper researches, and it will suffice me to have solely proved to you, by some examples, the possibility of establishing a general theory of the energetic arts.

You will find, perhaps, that what I have referred to analogy may equally be derived, in part, or totally, from physiological causes. In effect, the dilation of the organ of voice can explain the grave tone of admiration, and the contraction of the throat, caused by the blood, pushed with violence into the adjacent vessels, the sharp and cutting tone of choler. You would then have a new resemblance between the art of gesture and the theory of declamation, but of which the effect would not be an agreeable one. I mean to say, that resemblance which, by the number of phenomena, makes it difficult for us to decide if we ought rather to derive it from one source or from another : for the rest, we shall generally do best in adhering to that which will explain the thing with the greatest perspicuity. This advantage, in my opinion, appertains to the analogy relative to the phenomena reported above, and to others which resemble them. For the rest, it is not difficult to reserve the other modifications of the voice for physiological causes : for examples of this, I shall quote the smothered voice of fury, the profound sighs of sadness and of love, the trembling voice, sobbing and interrupted, of the dejection of grief. I ought still to make a passing remark, i. e. that the elevation of the voice, which ordinarily accompanies the last words of a question, is founded upon an intention or a design with motive. In discourse, there is always something similar to the tones of a chant. After many modulations, the ear is dissatisfied, unless the voice should fall back into this fundamental tone. He who puts a question, by terminating it in a different tone, forces (as one may say) the listener to terminate the incomplete music by his *own reply :* thus appeasing his wounded ears, hurt by the antimelodious suspension, at the same time that he is satisfying the curiosity of his interrogator.

To judge by these rules, so easy and so simple in appearance, you would not believe how much of abstracted matter they contain, so curious, and so complicated that it is with difficulty language supplies me with the terms I stand in need of. I am, indeed, already puzzled how to express my ideas in a manner clear, striking, and intuitive.

Withdraw, I pray, for a moment, your attention from the play of the gestures, and fix it upon the *rhythms* of discourse : you will remark three different kinds of it. We find an infinity of intermediate degrees where the ordinary language more or less approaches elevated declamation, as the latter approaches to the chant.

Each of these diverse species I have just been indicating has its determinate employ: the metre is only proper in certain cases ; for there are some where it would be displaced. In some situations of the soul it serves to reinforce the effect of the expression, which it would destroy or weaken in others.

What would be the calm and reflective discussion of a thinker on the cold recital of a historian in verse? What would become of a slight dialogue, passing successively from one sentiment to another, in a feeble and superficial tone, if it were reduced to strophes and antistrophes? What, finally, would be a discourse, although full of energy, dictated by friendship, or a recital of daily events, composed in lyrical metre, of a characteristical cadence and harmony? We reject similar productions as displaced, as out of nature.

Formerly, whilst history was the tradition of grand events and glorious facts, which fervid imagination and patriotic ardour endeavoured to immortalize; whilst philosophy was confined to bold fictions upon the origin of the Gods and the formation of the world, the one and the other might easily ally themselves to poetry, and become borrowers of all its finest ornaments: but when the Muse of history sunk to a calm and impartial recital, and philosophy began to occupy itself with cold and abstracted researches, then Herodotus in the one, and Pherecydes in the other, followed the impression of the good taste which induced them to prefer prose.

Yet even the prosaic tone of Pherecydes would become false, if, every time he reasons on an object, he did not elevate his style till he approached towards the majestic rhythm and the proud number of the inspired orator, since the thing is the same in the number of prose as in the metre of verse; for instance, would it not be false and ridiculous, if a letter of friendship or business should assume the soft and languishing style of the Elegies of Tibullus ? A similar letter ought doubtless to have a certain character of tenderness and amenity; the number and harmony ought equally to correspond with the nature of the predominant sentiment; but it is not necessary that it should be written with those sensibly noted cadences, with those soft and carefully selected measures, which constitute the charm of the prose of Gessner : without something above the vulgar, the style would be weary, stale, flat, and unprofitable.

The application of this remark to the different kinds of declamation makes *itself ;* the song full of sentiment, whatever be its character, ought not to be recited, but should be chanted. When even declaimed with the most exact expression, it would avail but little in my opinion : for we

can only feel the full charm of it whilst the simple sound becomes the musical tone, and when
the indecided rhythm is subjected by the measure.

But where is the man who could bear to hear,
without laughing (at least the first time), a letter
chanted—such as was the case in the ancient
French opera? The ridiculous becomes greater,
when the personage, without having often reread,
or written the letter himself, *receives it only.*
Notwithstanding, this circumstance would not
justify a letter in chant, since it then ceases to
be so, and becomes a song, an elegy, a romance,
addressed to a determinate personage. In the
mean time, my friend, let us return from this apparent digression to the veritable object now in
question.

The play of gesture has the same species, or,
if you like it better, the same degrees we have
distinguished above, in number and in declamation; all the expressions of the different situations
of the soul, which we have learned to know, elevate themselves by innumerable degrees, from
their origin, from the first suspicion of an affection, unto its entire developement. You will,
without doubt, recall the sketch I traced you of
joy under the appearance of rapture. Examine

once more the eye open and smiling, the arms extended to their full length, and the figure elevated upon the point of the foot, and floating as it were in the air, &c. and you will have the most decided, most complete expression of this affection : an expression you may *weaken* more than once without destroying it, or even without making it any longer *cognizable :* give a soft curve to the right line described by the arms, and, spite of this change, these will remain extended ; if one of the feet is more fixed on the earth, the other less elevated, and more near the former, the body will not the less exalt itself, and the step will be still light and floating.　If the eye contract, and the mouth close a little ; if the eye be brilliant, and the mouth more gently respire, the eyes will not be less open, the look will not be less lively, or the respiration less full.　*(See Plate* XXXIX.)

Make here a second and more considerable change : sink the arms lower on each side ; give less force to the muscles, so that the figure may insensibly elevate itself ; place the two feet lightly upon the earth, and make the edge of the teeth visible by a feeble and fugitive motion of the mouth, and you will yet have more than the expression of simple contentment : it *is* joy—but

joy either dawning or departing—in that point
of view, where it is equally ready to elevate itself
to a superior degree, or to sink into a perfect
calm.   *(See Plate* XL.)

Weaken the expression of the other affections
in the same manner ; for example, that of choler,
which grinds the teeth, and whose fury can hardly
be restrained within any due bounds : *(See Plate*
XLI.) or that of the most profound melancholy,
which, fixing its eyes on the earth, is sometimes
immovable, and at others slowly dragging along
its heavy pace.   *(See Plate* XLII.)   Here, as
before, retain the *species,* but not the total force
of the expression : let the one cast his arms less
before, and let the fist be closed, and the muscles
firmly stretched.   Let the head of the other be
less elevated, the arms more crossed, and his
hands hid in his habits, but less towards the superior part of the bosom, and I think you will
have a number of examples sufficiently large to
enable you to raise in the general the differences
which present themselves to my thought.   I
mean to say, the difference which there is between the expression entirely dreaded, achieved,
and supported, and that which is less complete,
less fixed, and susceptible of superior degrees : so
that, from this reason, it may vanish more easily,

adopt other shades, mingle and transform itself
into expressions of a different nature.

The art of gesture has its lyrical productions,
which excite enthusiasm, in which it elevates
itself to the highest degree of perfection, in
choosing movements the most complete and
best pronounced, so as to correspond completely
with the character of each passion.   In this case,
this art has the syllables and determined number
of metre; it is (as I may say) a music for the
organ of sight, as the other is a dance for the ear.
Represent to yourself, in the mean time, a dancer
executing a pantomime with miens and attitudes
more superficial and less decided, or with the in-
coherent and negligent movements of the actor,
and he will produce the same effect upon you as
a poet composing stupid and prosaic odes.   The
movements of such a pantomime will appear indolent to you; its expressions will be without
either soul or energy.   You require that he
should represent with earnestness the affections
with which he is supposed to be animated: you
wish it, in *joy*, to be lively, light, sparkling; that
he should almost float in the air, and apparently
only touch the earth as he bounds along: in the
full expression and delicious raptures of love, you
desire that his look should be soft and tender;

that the passion which carries him towards the beloved object should be mingled with a voluptuous languor; and that he should embrace that object with ecstasy. If it is the sentiment of pride which predominates in his mind, you demand that he should elevate himself with grandeur, darting around him looks of personal satisfaction; and that the contempt he entertains for another should make itself known by his grave pace, so measured as to make him occupy a greater space of ground as he moves majestically along, in such a manner as to compel you to lavish applauses on the pantomime, so much more lively, as he shall the more exceed your expectation in the attempt. Notwithstanding you require that the laws of beauty and propriety should not be violated, it is necessary for the body to elevate itself lightly, and without stiffness: the arms ought to spread from the right line: you wish that the opening of the eye and the mouth should not present the grimaces of an absurd mask: the languor of love ought not to degenerate into idiotism, nor its ecstasy to run into distortions.

You desire that contempt should not be pushed to a *real* disgust—but, *rightly governed,* the expression, carried to enthusiasm, would generally obtain your suffrage. In subjects which are not lyrical, that is to say, where the chant is not employed, but solely a more sustained declamation, as in the gesture of the impassioned orator or the inspired reader, you would disapprove, as misplaced and unnatural, those too determined motions which belong uniquely to the pantomime dancer. Notwithstanding it is permitted the orator and the rhapsodist to approach the more decided and complete shades of expression, accordingly as their discourses are more or less impassioned, their attitudes and their motions may be more developed, more sounded, and more sustained than those of the simple comedian: for he is absolutely confined to a free and light play, which, from time to time, may rapidly approach the full and entire expression of the affections, without its being permitted to be carried to the *highest point.* In truth, there may be characters where the actor by turns becomes lyrical poet, orator, and rhapsodist; and that, during these passages, he also borrows their play: but, during dialogue, properly so called, in the march of the essential action, his play ought to be easy, light, and natural:

he ought ever to confine himself to carrying the expression solely to a certain degree, and to indicate it simply, without imitating the orator in his movements, and still less the pantomime actor.

The parallel I have been establishing between the play of gesture and the number of discourse and declamation may have made you guess that I am not partial to pieces of the theatre written in *verse*. I am conscious that I have here many great examples against me—the judgment of whole nations and the critiques of very many literary men; but the greatest portion of the nation to which I have the honour to belong is on my side.

Tragedy in verse has long been disused in this country: we are disgusted with those swelling declamations and monotonous tirades which are inseparable from versification, and in which the poet is perpetually shining, at the expense of truth, of the interest and the progress of the action. We do not more approve that bombastic and unnatural play which is the general consequence of the poetical and oratorical developement of the sentiments.

We have not yet been able to manifest our

opinion in this respect, and to justify the preference we give to prose. It will not suffice to
declaim against that which is false, inflated, and
contrary to nature. This is not a demonstration, but a problem which remains to be demonstrated. Nevertheless, in my opinion, this demonstration appears very possible to me, in
further developing the nature of the drama, and
in comparing it with that of metre.

LETTER XXX.

On the different national Theatres — Predilection for the Ancients—Judgment of Aristophanes — Diderot — The dramatic Works of Dryden.

Do not tax me with injustice towards the French nor with prejudice for the English theatre : in truth, I do not merit either the one or the other of these reproaches. I grant that we have bombast and exaggeration in *London* as well as in *Paris;* but faults will still be faults, whether committed by a few or by a number of personages ; and if one man plays ill at Paris, it will not justify another for committing the same error in London. You are impatient to know what grounds I proceed upon, in deriving the proscription of versification from the theatre. In your mind, this literary dispute is exhausted: nevertheless you seem desirous that I should enter the lists.

One of the principal arguments resorted to by the partisans of versification is the example of the Greek and Roman authors. I am as far as any man from treating this just predilection for the ancients as a prejudice, notwithstanding I think that they may have their defaults in regard to versification. If the Greeks have been so perfect in each kind of poetry; if they appear so inimitable, it is because they were *creators*. Affectation and research of new beauties, which, in *general*, can neither conciliate themselves with the nature of the progression of ideas nor with the form and the effect proposed to be produced; nor, particularly, with the motive of the subject chosen, are the sole causes which hurt the species, and the particular production in each species. But this affectation is the work of imitators, who spoil all the kinds, wishing to become creators in their turns; and, to give themselves an air of originality, they strive to surpass their predecessors. In treating the particular subject of a species, they unnaturalize it; because, marching with a servile fear upon the steps of their predecessors and models, they take the slightest wandering for a gross fault. True genius is distracted, dazzled, or bewildered in false routes, by the attention bestowed on grand models, if its predecessors have transmitted any.

Nothing of this kind held good with the Greeks, who were the *inventors* of all the arts. As such they were originals, even in creating the

species in all their truth and simplicity. They
did not seek to reunite perfections incompatible
among themselves, and consequently they could
neither fail of an effect nor produce one less complete than another.   Their genius and sensibility
gave themselves totally up to their object, without respect to any model, for they had none ;
and, far from wishing to add foreign beauties,
they contented themselves in developing their
native powers.   Their work took all the forms
of which it was susceptible, and thus they approached Nature in the perfection of her productions, because they imitated the simplicity,
the liberty, and the vigour of her mode of operation.   This advantage disappeared, in posterior
times, from the moment there were models to
follow, and certain ideas of effect and perfection
had been adopted.   From thence it perhaps
comes, that the first works of the Greeks (at least
as far as we are capable of forming any judgment upon the subject) are also the most
perfect.

The dramatic poem was the only one which,
among the Greeks, did not follow the same
march as their other poetical productions.   It
did not develope of itself with unshackled liberty.
Grafted, from its origin, upon the lyrical species,

it borrowed from it its forms and manners, so that a kind of foreign taste ensued, which in truth lost itself a little in the course of time, but never entirely. This circumstance, which accompanied the birth of the theatre, was, without doubt, the reason why Eschylus is not elevated to the height that Sophocles attained by marching in his track. Besides, in the first works of the Greeks, their language was too florid, too epic, and too exalted; consequently its prosody, too unequal and too lyrical, could but ill adapt itself to ordinary dialogue. It was necessary then that the Greeks should long and laboriously search after that perfection they did not find at first : they *corrected* incessantly, until they had substituted a diction more simple and less overcharged to the epic style. According to the testimony of Aristotle, the advantage of the Iambic verse consisted in its nearer approach to prose.—(101. *See Aristot. Rhet.* l. iii. c. *3.*)

Following the sentiment of this philosopher, it is *prose* which is best adapted to a dramatic poem. If the Greeks had continued to improve their theatre, we may rationally suppose that, in preferring better to good, they would have substituted *prose*, even to a more prosaic *metre.* But they were governed by a prejudice equal to that which still retains our neighbours in subjection. No one had courage to banish versification totally from the scene which it had taken such strong possession of. Besides, it appeared to them that Sophocles had carried the art to the very highest degree of perfection, and that, after his sublime works, the attempt at producing any thing better was an impossibility.

Aristotle himself says *(De Poet I.)* " That, after many changes and revolutions, Tragedy reposed herself when she possessed all which was proper for her."—Nevertheless we must not silently pass over one important circumstance, which would not without difficulty have permitted the Greek poets the introduction of prose in their theatrical works. The question relates to the extraordinary grandeur of their theatres and the immense concourse of spectators. I shall cite a curious passage from a learned and ingenious Frenchman.

" Is it not very possible," says he, " that the great quantity of spectators it was necessary to be heard by, in spite of the confused murmur which they excited, even in moments of attention, occasioned the elevation of the voice, the detachment of the syllables, and the support of the pronunciation, by the aid of verse?—thus making the utility of Horace's observation experimentally known.

> ' Vincentem strepitus, et natum rebus agendis.'
> *Ad Pisones,* v. 82.

" It was commodious for the intrigue, and made itself audible through noise and tumult. But, was it not also a necessary consequence, that this exaggeration should extend itself, at the same time, and from the same cause, over the gait, the gestures, and all the other parts of action? whether poetry gave birth to theatrical declamation, that the necessity of this declamation sustained and introduced poetry and its emphasis upon the scene, or that this system, formed by little and little, had lasted, by the convenience of its parts, it is certain that all which is enormous in the dramatic art produced itself, and disappeared at the same time." —*Diderot.*

In the mean time, adopt that of these species of representations which shall most please you : that of Diderot or mine. The argument, founded upon the example of the ancients, will not be less weakened in either case.   If the ancients had not atttained the ideal perfection of the scene, it would follow that we ought to aim at surpassing rather than equaling them ; and if with them the versification was connected with certain foreign circumstances, it is necessary that one should cease the moment that the others no longer exist; for it would be folly to preserve a thing which might be as well dispensed with, and while the necessity which gave rise to its invention exists no longer.   If, by a natural consequence, we suppose that the theatrical play of the ancients was analogous to the rest of their dramatic system, and took a character more elevated and pompous, it neither ought nor can hold good with respect to the modern actors.   It is very easy for you to comprehend the advantages of these arguments. In truth, nothing is yet proved in favour of prose, but we may as fairly aver, that nothing has hitherto been proved against it; so that the two parties remain just as they were, if those who plead the cause of versification were not precisely attached to the overthrow of the principal argument alleged in favour of prose.   It is now above forty years since a German writer avowed

himself an advocate against the use of versification, which he considered as improbable and
unnatural. " For," said he, " those men, who
develope their thoughts without preparation,
cannot amuse themselves with reckoning up
syllables, and methodically disposing their discourse according to such or such a *measure*.
In a word, it is impossible for them to discourse
in verse without losing sight of nature and
probability."   A friend of the above writer
defends the use of verse with great vivacity—
he acknowledges the improbability, but stoutly
denies that a comedy in verse is inferior to one
written in prose; because there does not exist
any production of art, whatever be its kind,
which does not offend against probability in
some way or other. " Comedy itself, without
speaking of versification (says he), has other faults
of that nature, which we do not simply *tolerate*,
but expressly demand. No one requires a strict
and scrupulous imitation of nature; good taste
would be wounded by it. It is a general rule
for each artist not to render his work so perfect
a resemblance to his original that it cannot be
distinguished from it by some mark or other.
Now, in comedy, versification is precisely the

most happy mode that can be employed to distinguish the *imitation* of the events of life from the actual reality of such occurrences.   By versification we distinguish the copy from the original, and this method serves to flatter the ear in the most agreeable manner."

None of the posterior apologists of versification have given reasons preferable to those I have just been *quoting*.   Those of Hurd have neither so much weight or delicacy ; so that I do not recollect any one who has combated them in a victorious way.   On the contrary, the reasonings of the critics seem to be as favourable to the cause of versification, as the sentiments of the amateurs of the drama appear to be on the other side of the question.

If prose, by hazard, sometimes obtains the preference, it is solely because much more perfection is looked for in the style of the poet than in that of the prosaic author: that the perfections of the drama ally themselves with difficulty to a flowing, easy versification, and, after all, the simple pleasure of the ear neither merits the sacrifice of the sublime beauties nor the infinite pains it costs the poet to express them in fine verses . . . . You see that this rea-

soning assumes all the advantages to versification.
But is the cause of prose really so weak that
we must yield to arguments like these? The
plays of Dryden are mostly written in verse,
and contain many undoubted beauties; but let
any candid reader take them up, and, after an
impartial perusal, give an unbiased opinion: he
will then, most probably, declare that the necessity of adhering to metrical precision has compelled the author into that bombast and, not unfrequently, ludicrous style which provokes laughter instead of pathos and sublimity. Shakspeare
is never so little effective as when he jingles in
rhyme—he was the Heaven-fired bard of nature,
and when he left her track, he was shackled and
perplexed. Had verse been *natural* to the drama,
the poet of Avon would indubitably have ex-
celled in it.

There has been a comedy lately written in
blank verse, which has been received with merited
success: had the attempt been made in rhyme,
its effect would hardly have been crowned with
an equal portion of approbation. The comedy
referred to is the Honey-Moon. The subject
is not a new one, but it is elegantly handled,
and reflects the highest honour on the memory

of its departed author.   Enough on the subject of prose and versification for the present : when a fit opportunity occurs, I may perhaps renew the argument—an argument superfluous, perhaps, as it relates to the British drama, but connected with the essence of theatrical writing in general.   Adieu for the present.

LETTER XXXI.

*On Versification—Descriptive Poetry—Dramatic Poetry—
Remarks thereon.*

THE poet does not imitate for the sole pleasure
of imitating; the first merit of his work does not
essentially consist in the most perfect resemblance
to nature, but in the greatest effect it is capable
of producing: and, not to fail of this effect, it is
permitted him to wander from the original in his
imitation.   Here we are of one mind : we wish
every thing to be retrenched which can either
hurt or weaken the effect, and all to be superadded
which can favour or augment it.   But I am ap-
prehensive lest we should often have too general
an idea of this effect, and that a number of things
should appear more indifferent and more insignificant than they really are.   Every poet has the
hope of giving pleasure for his end : but how
infinitely may the kinds of this pleasure be multiplied ?   That which is fit for the one is often
incompatible with the other.   The seasoning
which gives a zest to *one* dish will often render

another insipid : the beauties generally compatible with the idea of a poem may nevertheless be contradictory to a particular species of poesy, where the pleasure of the soul ought to be the result of a determinate kind of occupation. Thus every thing which destroys this ought necessarily to destroy the other. Let us not, therefore, be eager to conclude that all poems must be written in verse, because the principal aim of the poet is to please ; and that the effect of versification consists in producing pleasure. Let us rather previously inquire, if versification have not some particular property which constrains one agreeable occupation of the soul as much as it facilitates another. Versification is not, as it is generally believed, a thing of pure agreement; it must not be considered simply as a pleasing organ, of which the full, pure, and round tone renders the pronunciation more clear and more sonorous, and which becomes valuable, for this reason, to all sorts of declamation. Versification of itself disposes to declamation ; it favours and invites the employment of it ; it gives more of character, more of energy to the discourse, and serves, in the mean time, as a mode to elicit the sense and sentiment in a manner more brilliant and more striking : every metre is an imitation of a characteristical progress of ideas, with their developement. It answers, then, to a certain particular species of sentiment and situation of soul, in always preserving its proper character, now more concealed, and now more strongly expressed : in one of these metres adopted by poetry, we cannot mistake gentleness, softness, and languor. One or two passions are full of fire and energy, whilst a third is distinguished by a tone majestic and severe: this is rapid and unequal, the other slow and dragging; while one exalts, the other depresses the soul. In one word, their movements are equally hurried, soft, or pompous, according to their respective properties. For this reason, the choice of metre cannot be a thing indifferent to the poet, who ought carefully to select it according to the effect he wishes to produce, and his work will, more or less, fall short of its effect, as this selection happens to be lucky or unfortunate.

In the mean time, figure to yourself a metre composed entirely of measures, perhaps of *uniform* rhymes, and you will not be long in acknowledging that their employ can contribute infinitely in augmenting the effect of a lyrical poem, or of a didactic or descriptive kind. But would the same thing hold good in a dramatic

work ?   A single sentiment predominates in the
soul of the lyrical poet, whether this sentiment
be of joy, love, or pride.   In a word, one of
those affections of which the progression is equal,
regular, and uniform.   What means can the poet
employ more natural and more calculated to produce the same sentiment in the soul of the auditor,
than that of a suite of syllables of a uniform
measure, and rigorously adapted to the progression of this sentiment ?   In verses of equal measure, or followed regularly by a shorter verse, the
cadence of which exhausts, without effort, the
hitherto sustained respiration (the indolence and
softness of the trochee), will best suit the soft
sentiment which predominates in the languishing
strain of the elegiac poet: a sentiment which,
from its beginning to its end, developes itself in
a slow and uniform manner, without sudden wan-
derings and unexpected transitions.

Impressions analogous to the march of ideas
produced by the poet upon the senses of the
auditor will then determine in his soul an equal
succession of the same ideas.   In descriptive
poesy, when the artist poet, after having considered his subject under all its different aspects,
preserves an impression, as lively as durable, of
astonishment or of a sympathetic charm—-then

how much may a well chosen and well wrought
measure augment and heighten the effect of the
picture? And in the didactic poem, when the
indignation with which the poet pursues the vices
entirely fills, at the same time that the sentiment
of the grandeur, the importance and sublime
character of the truths which he announces,
directs all his faculties to one single object, the
choice of proper metre cannot fail of giving a
double energy to his labours.

If, in the one or the other kind of these poems,
certain gradations present themselves,—slight
admixtures of foreign sentiments, or digressions,
interesting to be employed, it is easy to make use
of them with effect, whether by the measure and
harmony of proper words, well chosen phrases,
the skilful distribution of the cesura, by little
irregularities, managed with art and design, or
by a different arrangement of the periods. I
grant that it is neither natural nor probable,
that a heart full of any sentiment whatsoever, or
that a mind occupied in researches after important truths should attach itself with so much
attention to the mechanical parts of speech.
Nevertheless it must, at the same time, be confessed, that the happy employment of this very
measure (provided that the labour be artfully

and gracefully hid) infinitely contributes to augment the effect; and to produce effect is the first
concern of the poet.

The dramatic writer finds himself in a very
different position. Let any one endeavour to
discover the essential properties of this species of
poesy, and he will instantly acknowledge that in
tragedy, as well as in comedy, the soul ought not
to be affected with *one*, but with *many* sentiments;
the variety of which, managed by happy transitions and oppositions, makes the whole beauty of
dramatic composition, at the same time that it
ensures their effect. But if this be the good the
dramatic author ought to propose to himself, it
remains to know if it be advantageous to him to
subject himself to an invariable metre during the
whole course of his work.

The ancients, who appear to have understood
this matter better than the moderns, took care
not to employ a regular metre in their pieces:
they varied it, without any hesitation, every-
where where the change of the nature of a passion seemed to require it.

Quintilian blames Terence for not having
constantly employed the iambic verse of six
feet :

" In comœdia maxime claudicamus . . . licet
Terentii scripta ad Scipionem Africanum refe-
rantur : quæ tamen sunt in hoc genere elegan-
tissima, et plus adhuc habitura gratiæ, si inter
versos trimetros stetissent."

But with what bitter raillery has Bentley
treated this critique :

" Mirificum sane magni rhetoris judicium !
Crederes profecto, hominem nunquam scenam
vidisse, nunquam comœdum partes suas agentem
spectavisse.   Quid voluit ?   Quod nec Menander
nec ullus Græcorum fecit, Terentius ut faceret ?
*Ut Ira, metus, exultatio, dolor, gaudium, et quietæ
res et turbatæ, eodem metro lente agerentur ?* Ut
tibicen paribus tonis, perpetuoque cantico spec-
tantium aures vel delassaret vel offenderet ?"—
In Præfat. ad Terent.

It appears to me, that Quintilian might be
justified, though Bentley certainly is right, in
maintaining that to subject the expression of so
many affections, diametrically opposite to each
other, is to sin against probability.   I do not
deny but that declamation may so diminish this

fault, as to render it nearly insensible. I have myself heard several of the actors on the French stage practise this art with very happy success. But, much as I have admired their excellence in this respect, I always thought it a great hardship on them to be compelled to pay attention to words and syllables, when the soul ought to be wholly abandoned to sentiments of grandeur and expansion.

The modern poets, of all the countries of Europe, appear to have paid more respect to the opinions of *Quintilian* than to the examples set them by *Sophocles* and *Menander*.

LETTER XXXII.

Continuation of the Remarks on the Dramatic and the Epic Writer.

THE remark that the epic poet appears personally on the scene, while the dramatic poet, on the contrary, hides himself behind the personages he brings forward on the stage, is as ancient as it has been little examined, as to the consequences which flow from it. I wish to give you my ideas on the best mode of explaining this remark. In the epic poem, it is only one person who recounts the suite of events which make the object of the poem.—Previous to the communication of his ideas, he has already conceived, classed, and embellished them, so that no other object occupies either his mind or his heart, even in the actual moment of recital. The dramatic poem, on the contrary, presents personages, who, in each situation of import, find themselves in the real embarrassment of persons who communicate their ideas at the moment they receive them ; and their affections at the instant they are affected by their impressions ; so that, far from being solely occupied in expressing these sentiments and these ideas, they always tend to a determined mark, and constantly break forth, by the thought, into the future, continually experiencing modifications and changes often contrary in their interior and exterior situations, whether by their own proper actions, or by foreign impulsions.   In the recital, we hear a witness speak, who embraces the whole suite of events which he is recounting at a glance; he has a right to reject all details of an unimportant nature; he is permitted to give solely the *result* of long discourses, of entire series of varied sentiments, and of long reflections, which while they occupied the souls of his heroes, were often accompanied with embarrassment and disquietude.   When he makes his personages speak, he is not interdicted from shortening their discourse, and giving the body of it, provided that he does not alter its *essentials*.   In short, like a witness who recalls *things* more than *words*, he may lend his own expressions to his personages, in always characterising their discourse by the principal sentiment which belongs to each situation.   It is not thus in the drama.   In the moment of action we also hear the characters themselves speaking : for them the present moment is real—the future uncertain.   They present themselves to our regards, in each situation, under the forms proper to their characters, with the most slight modifications of the soul, and with those impressions, feeble or fugitive, which, during the developement of an intrigue, the continual reaction of the one upon the other produces alternately and without any interruption; their sentiment, always conformable to the situation, constantly shows itself just as it is:—feeble or impetuous at its birth; imperious in its progress; mastered sometimes, or half extinguished; hid for a moment, to reappear with greater force here-after.   In one word, none of these shades are lost for the spectator; and under his eyes the personages form, abandon, resume, modify, reject, or adopt the projects which the events, or the circumstances by which these events are ac-companied, seem to require or command.   All the characteristical traits, which distinguish the personages of a dramatic poem from those of every other poem, may be presented to the mind in one single idea, which is that of their actual presence and reality before our eyes; and it is the imposition of this magic upon our imagina-tion which constitutes the sole effect of the dramatic poem.   The pleasure which it ought to cause is visibly founded on this complete knowledge of the manners, intrigue, and catastrophe of an action, the talent of the dramatic poet, in familiarizing the spectator with the characters of the personages, who, from one moment to the other, manifest themselves according to their individual qualities, as well as upon the more intimate interest which the spectator takes in the lot of the characters who ought to excite it; an interest which can only have place in all its plenitude, when accompanied with a complete knowledge of all their propensities and most secret sentiments, as also all the details of the situations of their souls, and the state of circumstances, which can have any influence and effect upon them.

This granted, I call to your recollection the rule, that the poet, in general, ought to avoid every thing which can weaken effect, and diligently to cultivate all which can contribute to its success. In making this application to the dramatic poet, the result will be, that he should never substitute any circumstance in his imitation which can hinder the idea of reality, and much less any thing which may destroy that idea. All changes which he can permit himself to make in the subject he treats of, to augment the effect of it, avoid tedious details, give birth to interest-

ing characters and situations, never ought to
carry any injury to that illusion which makes us
think that we are really witnesses of the trans-
actions which are represented before us: on the
contrary, it is necessary that these changes should
always be subordinate to the situation of the
moment, to the ideas they are to develope, and
to the sentiments and designs which they give
birth to. Our soul has in itself a sentiment
which is never deceptive: she searches to find
her own proper nature in others, and cannot
accomplish this metamorphosis but inasmuch as
it there recognises its own essential properties.
Complete deviation from that which, according
to its sentiment, is uniquely true, necessarily
must destroy the impression which the soul
should receive: a slighter deviation will render
this impression slow, feeble, and confused.   Let
us consequently be cautious of rejecting from
the drama every thing which can offer the least
contradiction, or the slightest disagreement with
its essence: let us banish from it every thing
which the soul could not itself experience, in
taking the situation of the personages according
to the different positions in which they are placed
upon the scene: let us suppress all those sentiments in which its nature refuses to partake, and

which give birth to obstacles and difficulties incompatible with the laws which direct the exercise of its proper faculties : in the mean time, you will allow me, my friend, to transform some observations, of which I have great need, into so many questions ; for it is only in taking for a judge the interior and incorruptible opinion of each man, exempt from prejudice, that we are able to arrive at the truth of the observations we can make upon what passes in our souls.

Thus do you not find that each degree of sentiment, which ought not to have place at the *moment*, or perhaps *never*, disgusts and shocks you as much as if you should perceive an effect without a cause ? Do you not equally find that *outré* tones hurt you, when the character and situations of the personages demand a less degree of energy ? Now if, in the dramatic poem, moments of disorder are frequently replaced by instants of tranquillity ; if, often, things the most cold and indifferent in themselves ought to be said, not by secondary personages, but by the principals of the piece, the necessary effects of each passionate and displaced tone will be to destroy your pleasure, or what amounts to the same, the *illusion*, without which the pleasure cannot take place ? Would not too great an equality do injury to the essential merit of dramatic works, to the exact developement, and to the beautiful gradation of the sentiments?

Do you not find that there is never a brisk passage from a state of quietude and indifference to an affection entirely decided; that it is necessary to excite many shocks, and rouse many vibrations, successively more strong, to impress on the soul a movement uniform and determinate, whatever be their kind?

In observing your own self with a little attention, do you not remark that this determinate march of the ideas only takes place in the soul, while she embraces with all possible energy a single interesting object, and no foreign idea employs its other faculties? That the sentiment cannot fully occupy the soul, when the head is engaged by some project, or while the judgment searches and examines the means of arriving at its ends? These secondary perceptions diminish the energy of the principal sentiment, in causing a thousand admixtures, a number of deviations, incompatible with that open, frank, and certain progression which I have made mention of above, every sentiment having an opposite and counteracting force :—As, for example, it is impossible to hurry rapidly from the eagerness of choler to the soft

languor of love; in like manner as a clouded
sky requires time ere it can assume a pure and
cloudless azure; or an enraged sea assume a
smooth and glassy surface. Consequently, if we
consider the continual mobility of the sentiments
in the dramatic poem, every thing which con-
tradicts the regular progression of nature, every
sudden and violent transition from one sentiment
to another, will impede the effect, and destroy
the illusion, precisely because the spectator will
not be able to follow these rapid mutations with
equal celerity. I flatter myself that these remarks, and the observations upon which they
are founded, will appear striking and true to
you. I have also one more to add, which is,
that the number of the discourse, and the situation of the soul, are constantly in the most perfect harmony; that a certain determinate metre
constantly indicates a certain determinate sentiment, and cannot be in collision with that we
propose to indicate or excite, without the sentiment being either weakened or disturbed. Consider this remark, and the question, whether the
dramatic poet ought to write in prose or in verse
will be decided. If he writes the whole of his
piece in verse, he will often shock good taste, in
rendering nothing of importance · by the shifts

of language, a double danger awaits him : a discourse too common for verse, or a verse too
elevated for common discourse.   By the uniformity of his numbers, he will give too decided
a determination to his sentiment, and by this
means deprive himself of one of the greatest
beauties of which dramatic painting is susceptible, which consists in the delineation of the sentiments so that they may combine and strengthen
others, or diminish and destroy them.   If the
dramatic poet does not write the whole of his
piece in verse, there will always remain an interval between the verse and the prose, and the
metre will almost every where give a determination to the march of the ideas; which, in the
situation of the moment, the personage cannot
have, or at least cannot preserve; a determination
which will ever be false, if, in experiencing a
sentiment, it is necessary, in the mean time, to
weigh means and motives, or conceive and execute plans or schemes.   In the midst of the
intrigue, in the tumult of the action, at the birth
of the sentiments, at the changes, and at their
separation, they are merely approximations.   If,
as we ought, we wish to establish any harmony
between the sentiments and the number, the
number can only be attained by approaches,

which can only be accomplished by a metre
unconstrained, and a free, unfettered rhythm, a
mixture which prose alone can offer. Thus that
which I have wished to prove, I mean the necessity of the employment of prose, is founded on
the very idea of a dramatic poem. The reasons
which I have given are general; they are equally
opposite to a metre uniform and invariable, as to
one which is mixed with syllables of an unequal
measure. That which I have deduced in detail,
in my former letter, more particularly relates to
the first of these metres, because a uniformity of
syllables cannot be fit for the expression of sentiments, which are constantly varying; and I
have alleged against the last, that its hurried
transitions would be contrary to the duration
and the successive developement of the ideas:
each too sudden variation, in a metre once determined, is disagreeable, because it troubles and
arrests the soul in its operations. We lose the
advantage of anticipating the discourse of the
characters; we are deceived, we are lost, we are
deprived of that unconstrained freedom, with
which we delight to trace and follow the ideas
as they present themselves. This is precisely
(as I think) the meaning of Quintilian, and it
would be thus that I should reply to Bentley, as
to the more free metre, which admits not only

many cesuras, but several different kinds of feet also. I shall first of all ask, how it is to be employed? Would you adopt a metre so little characterised, and which resembles prose as much as the Iambic verse of six feet, and then permit the poet to dispose of his cesuras *ad libitum;* to mix the Iambics with what kind of feet he wishes, even not to heed a few extraordinary feet? It would be only necessary to carry this liberty to a certain degree, and we shall have verses whose metre will be recognised with difficulty, and which only forced corrections, like those of Bentley, would render sensible. Does any one, on the contrary, desire to adhere to a metre which is subjected to a certain number, and a certain quantity of feet? I shall then repeat the same question: how will any one pretend to order it so that it shall not be confounded or mistaken? or, if this is possible, would it not be a useless labour to make verses which should not have a better effect than prose? Let us choose a metre which really has its proprieties, and requires a rigorous management. This metre will always preserve its commanding tone: it will then be necessary to see, whether the effect of the scenic illusion would not be enfeebled by the employment of a similar measure?

That the epic poem may make use of this

measure admits not of a doubt.   The action
embraced in one point of view gives an impression determinate and permanent : arising at a
certain general tone, it seldom quits it, though,
during the several parts of the poem, the shades
may be more or less strongly marked ; and as
the epic poet wishes his auditor to contemplate
the subject in the same point of view with himself, as he possesses the right of retrenching
every thing which can render his verse cold, of
contracting uninteresting details, in changing the
dialogues of his characters, &c. an unique and
permanent tone may, therefore, be very well calculated for the success of his work.   But how
can a similar tone be adapted for the exertions
of the dramatic poet, since he makes his personages act for themselves, according to their
different characters and interests ; for whom the
present alone exists, while the veil which covers
the *future* is scarcely uplifted ; who can never
experience sensations following the impressions
which the *aggregate* of the actions shall produce,
but simply pursuing the impulsion of the solitary
events of their respective situations, and whom
the difference of their characters and their interests do not permit to be equally affected ?

After all I have been saying, I mean to con-

clude, that a dramatic poem in verse is a less
perfect work than one written in prose; for if
(according to the best given definition of a poem)
the essence consists in the sensible perfection of
discourse, doubtless one of the conditions will
be, that every thing should be in the most exact
accord; and that the number should consequently tally in the most rigid manner to the
sense of the words, and the sense of the words
to the actual situation of the characters on the
stage.

Furthermore, I think we might aver, that it
is infinitely less easy to write a piece for the
theatre in prose than in verse. He who has
made the trial will more justly appreciate the
difficulties it is to overcome in painting an unin-
terrupted series of sentiments by discourse, so
that *each* shall have its just proportion of force,
its proper duration, and its essential traits, without the admission of any incoherencies or too
rapid transitions: but since a discourse pursued
in verse does not resemble ordinary language,
the metre imperceptibly makes us glide over
many things contrary to nature. The deficiency
of several shades of fine touches and adroit pre-
parations is hidden by the magic harmony of
verse: the language insensibly elevates itself to a

more noble tone. As the diction ought to be equal, this extraordinary difficulty, which the prose writer must vanquish to find the most true expression, neither too elevated, too strong, too common, nor too weak, entirely disappears with respect to the poet; because he rolls perpetually, in a narrow circle of words, proper to the tone he has chosen; and more, the derangement of the order in which the thoughts develope themselves, cross, destroy, and then reappear with greater verity, is much less sensible in versification than in prose. And this order, which, in all the dramas where it is scrupulously observed, charms the mind as well as the heart of the spectator, is never perfectly seized but by truly inspired genius. I have too good an opinion of your penetration, my friend, to think it needful to make a detailed application of this reasoning upon *number* to the play of *gesture*.

You doubtless recollect the parallel which I have established between all the musical arts: thus, the general value of my principles will not escape you. In truth, my limits will not allow me to be more diffuse.

LETTER XXXIII.

Apology for the Chant of the Opera—The Grecian Drama
—Obligation on the Comedian to conform himself to the
Spirit of the Poet—Answer to the Question, whether the
Sacred Orator may borrow from the Comedian, and how
far such Studies may be allowed him?

ARE the eulogies you lavish on the principles by
which I combat the drama written in verse sin-
cere or ironical? You find much curious matter
in these speculations. Provided you do not contest the truth, I consent that you should call
them subtile.

I ought to observe that *number* is only a simple supplement added to the general effect of
a drama, and that a similar supplement may
appear weak, without our being able to deny it
any effect whatever. We know that the most
strong cord is essentially nothing more than a
collection of slight fibres, which an infant may
tear in pieces; but that these fibres, combined
together, are sufficient to chain a Hercules. An

attentive examination proves to us that our
most energetic sensations, our most lively pleasures are only the results of trifling circumstances, which, each taken separately, appear
feeble and insignificant, but whose activity is,
rightly searched, not less real.   The fear with
which my reasoning against the versification of
the drama inspires you, with regard to the opera,
explains to me a circumstance which I have not
before comprehended : I mean the zeal, I might
almost say the passion with which you have
pleaded the cause of pantomimical representations.   With you, music is the first of the arts,
and you openly manifest your contempt of a
critique which, by cold subtilties, would banish
this charming art from the scene, and thus exhaust the principal source of your pleasures.
Certainly this critique, if such be its intent, is
but little indulgent : but are you not too severe,
my friend, in suspecting it of so little politeness
towards you ?   Have not many proofs of indul-
gence towards pantomime been evinced, and
ought you to expect the same lenity in favour of
the opera ?   It is true that if less characteristical
metres and oratorical declamations ought to be
rejected from the drama, by a much stronger

reason the lyrical metre, of *which* the character is so marked, and the declamation carried to the highest pitch (I mean the chant) ought to be equally proscribed: but this chant, which renders the lyrical metre necessary, has so much of softness, it binds the most voluptuous sense of the soul with such delicious fetters, causes it to be affected with such magical sensations, that we pay not the least attention to the defect of harmony which there is between the expression and the real situation of the soul, nor to the effect lyrical, substituted for the effect dramatic. The truth of the action is weakened, and consequently the *effect* is equally so: but what is lost with regard to the soul is regained on another side. Multiplied beauties amply compensate for this deficiency of truth. The very vices of the plan, the incoherency of the events, the faulty expressions of sentiment and number disappear, and the pearls hide the poorness of the thread on which they are ranged, by the potent art of the musician. An effect so powerful cannot be by any means placed in comparison with that which is produced by simple metre. The principal force of this consists in its harmony with the situation of the soul: at every time where this harmony is deficient, in the dramatic poem, there no longer remains any thing more than that pleasure which a cadence and regular harmonies procure for the organs of *hearing;* and this pleasure is too feeble and too cold to prevent our sense of the least deviation from truth, or to be able to repair its loss. You will doubtless tell me that, notwithstanding this, there are many pieces written in verse, which are extremely affecting, and I willingly agree with you; but I ask you, in my turn, what is the cause of the interest which these pieces inspire? Banish from the opera all that is false, and the effect will be diminished: banish what is false from a declaimed drama, and its effect will be augmented. The rather hazardous opinion, which I have ventured on the subject of the drama of the Greeks, has displeased you, and you have endeavoured to justify its versification, because this drama was a species of opera, and that its sustained declamation bore some resemblance to the chant. I confess that this circumstance ought not to have escaped me: had I made mention of it, I should have expressed myself, perhaps, with more reserve and circumspection, but not with more precision

than you have done. I should not have refused
the Greeks the true idea of dramatic poems, but
solely that of the simple drama, which appertains not to any foreign art, and whose effect is
produced by its own proper means; and in this
manner the proposition, which it imported me to
establish, remains in all its force, *i. e.* that the
example of the Greeks ought to be no model for
us; because, versification was founded among
this people, on their own particular ideas of the
drama, or that the art which they associated to
it rendered this versification necessary, and that,
from the moment of their separation, it became
not only superfluous, but even hurtful to the
effect. You make two objections concerning
the too general rule which prescribes the moderation of theatrical action. I do not hesitate to
acknowledge the justice of the first : in fact, the
actor ought to conform himself to the intention
of the author, and when he has written his
drama in verse, or, to speak with more precision,
has chosen a strongly characteristical metre, and
when the entire tone of the diction ought to be
elevated with the number, it then, doubtless,
becomes necessary that the play, as well as the
language, should swell into proportionate dig-

nity. A French critic (Diderot) has said, that in acting——

" Il falloit outrer tout ou rien."

This may perhaps prove to you, that my attack on versification (sometimes the necessary and at others the accidental source of error) is not out of place. I have endeavoured to cut up the evil by the root, and I should have given a proof of imprudence had I addressed my counsels to the actors without taking some notice of the poets as I proceeded.

It appears to me that your second remark must be grounded upon some misunderstanding. The observation that, with certain people, that is natural and simple which would appear affected and *outré* with us, is not to the purpose.

Is there not (I shall ask in my turn), among these lively people you may have in view, the least difference between the oratorical gesture, the play of conversation, and the dance ? Do we not find some limits between the chant, elevated declamation, and the ordinary tone of society ?——no separation between verse, majestic rhythm, and the easy and familiar number peculiar to dialogue ?

If these differences encounter each other, and, in effect, exist universally, and principally amongst the more polished people, it by no means follows, from your observation, that the play of the drama ought not always to contain itself in certain limits. This only results from it, that the same limits do not constantly serve for the same people; that this play shall have more fire, more energy among the one, and that it may be more cold, more feeble, and less expressive among others. This conducts us to a fresh remark; *i. e.* that the whole merit of an actor can only be appreciated in his own country: in the midst of those whose manners he imitates, and whose customs he has observed: thus, he can only appear with his true eclat upon his national theatre, and seldom on a foreign one. Thus, as you see, I apply not your remark concerning the true warmth and fiery dispositions of certain people to that fallacious and affected play, which the public of another nation are so partial to. I presume that you do not pretend to call that play natural which bad taste and bad critics have introduced on some theatres.

I shall terminate this suite of abstracted remarks by adding one to them, which, in truth, does not arise from an observation of yours; but will, I trust, not displease you. It has been asked, whether it be allowable for the sacred orator to form himself on the modes of the theatre, and if it be allowable in him to adopt the same principles of tone and gesture? Not long ago this question was debated with considerable warmth. For my own part, I shall answer, that it is, and that it is not, according to circumstances: it is not, inasmuch as the thoughts and the characters of the greater portion of parts cannot, by any means, accord with the thoughts and the character of the sacred orator; and secondly, because the drama and sermon are so widely distinct that the action proper for one can rarely be so for the other. The persons of the drama utter thoughts which owe their existence to the situation of the moment: the preacher communicates those to the people which he has had full leisure to class and arrange in his mind. The actors are in a condition of inquietude, real and exterior, uncertain and irresolute; they are agitated by diverse sentiments and by various ideas. The exterior tranquillity of the preacher is not disturbed in any way; he has

only one grand, principal, and permanent sentiment, which he is at liberty to develope at his
leisure. In the soliloquy of Hamlet upon suicide, the object is of the most momentous importance; the soul is mounted to a serious tone;
this tone and attitude may assume the greatest
dignity. May the sacred orator make use of
similar expressions? Certainly not, because
Hamlet, buried in his reflections, is only seriously commencing the examination of the question. In passing from one idea to the other, he
loses himself in the labyrinths of doubt, which
multiply in his mind; a situation which could
never be decent in an orator, encharged with
the task of fixing and guiding the judgment of
the public.

When, however, the sentiment is decidedly in
favour of virtue, truth, and morality, what should
hinder the preacher from making the theatre his
school, or an accomplished actor his model? To
bind down the preacher to a simple motion of
his hands, insignificant, and employed by chance,
is to rob him of that advantageous power of
persuasion, in the most solemn and interesting
concern of man's temporal and future felicity,
which is allowed to the lawyer at the bar, when

defending an action of the most trivial and unimportant nature.

There is one reserve, however, which a preacher is at all times bound to pay attention to : even when he is most expressive he should be moderate; when most affecting, he should preserve his dignity, and be particularly cautious of wandering into that extravagance which must ever be disgusting and unbecoming the serious and sublime concern of which he has to treat.

LETTER XXXIV.

Concerning the Study of Characters—Monologue—Whether the Success of a Piece be any real Proof of its Merit.

Your questions are of importance : the actor certainly ought to study his own character with a view to its connexion with the others, as by this double study he will acquire the tone and perfect knowledge of his own particular part. Without this attentive view of the *ensemble,* without this exact appreciation of the portion which a particular character carries in the aggregate of a drama, without this modest and voluntary information, the effect of the play, if it is not entirely destroyed, is at least greatly weakened and defaced.   Horatio, perceiving the spectre of Hamlet's father at the very time it is presented to the eyes of the prince, might, by vehemence of attitude and action, not merely *divide,* but attract the *sole* attention of the spectators to himself: then he would compel Hamlet to a bare imitation, or to an exaggerated and

unnatural expression of his surprise. I know
that many difficulties oppose themselves to this
perfection; the rage for novelties in the direc-
tors, the false taste of the actors, who, eager to
dazzle, frequently prefer the acclamations of the
multitude to the eloquent silence of the connoisseur.

If each particular character ought to be studied according to its connexion with the *ensemble*
of the piece, it is equally necessary that the actor,
in the study of the scenes, should never lose sight
of the general idea of his part.

Enlightened by the comparison of his particular proportions, he will learn to restrain or
give loose to his feelings by science and by
rule : one passage may contain much scope for
warmth and passion, but in such or such a
scene there may perhaps chance to be another
still more highly coloured; so that if he exhausts
his energies in the first scene of his part, he will,
most probably, be languid and ineffective in the
last.

Suppose that a brother, witness of the despair
of a beloved sister abandoned by the object of
her affections, swears, by all that is sacred, to
avenge her cause on the perfidious youth, and
that the actor, charged with this part, should

declaim the imprecation with too much violence; there would remain no distinguishing mark of passsion, when, encountering the object of his vengeance——he has to charge him with his injuries in person.

Nevertheless, this fear of exhausting the powers ought not to be carried too far by the actor, as it might destroy the effect of his own part as well as the *ensemble* of the play.   For if he languishes through four acts to give effect to the fifth, the loss to the spectators is inadequate to the gain.   This is a very favourite scheme of our actors, and I have seen some of them jump from one extreme to the other, without any apparent cause or motive; as the thunder, which we have heard in feeble murmurs at a distance, will sometimes, when we least expect it, roll over our heads in all its noise and fury.   Doubtless, these strokes are louder, but, instead of making an impression, they only serve to *stun* us, whilst preparatory ones, and following each other in just gradations, impress the soul with fear——the mind with terror.

With regard to such plays as are represented on the stage, I have many reasons for judging them in the closet rather than in the theatre.   I agree with you, that the reader ought to be a

man gifted with every qualification; that he
should not only be endowed with an ardent imagination, but should add to that advantage a
refined and exquisite sensibility : a man who,
always alive to the scene, does not confine himself to keeping the dramatis personœ in his
thoughts, but who sees them present, and acts
their several parts in his own imagination, as he
proceeds.

The remark has been frequently made, that
such or such a piece produces a good effect, because its mediocrity is in the most perfect harmony with that of the actors, and that many
beautiful passages are lost in others, because
they stand in need of a Garrick to feel and to
express them.

Would it not be the height of injustice to
prefer the mediocre to the great poet, because
the representatives of the characters of the latter
were unable to do justice to his writings ? This
would be as false a judgment as to despise the
sublime compositions of Handel, because an
ignorant musician had shocked our ears by his
execrable mode of playing them.

LETTER XXXV.

On Approach and Removal—On Choler—Joy—The Transition from Jealousy to Love.

YOUR attention must now be carried to the progressive march of the passions, on which the merit of the candidate for dramatic fame must generally repose. When the affections resemble each other in the march of the ideas, they approach, and, *vice versa*, recede when this is not the case. Before I proceed, I wish you to contemplate four plates, where I have attempted to delineate the progressive march of inattention to a sort of climax, or curiosity and eagerness: you will thus perceive that, in every different shade, one object approaches nearer to the other.

These figures represent a lawyer reading a will to a client, who had no vehement expectations from the result:—*Plate* XLIII, I think, delineates this tolerably correctly. The lawyer, in *Plate* XLIV, has just come to the part where the name of the client is mentioned:—you will immediately see that he is drawing nearer. In

Plate XLV, you will see him approximating, with his mouth opened by expectation and all the eager avidity of curiosity. In the last instance *(Plate* XLVI.) he is so absorbed in his own concerns, and so delighted by the intelligence conveyed to him that he is in the very act of embracing the attorney.

You will thus find that the affections succeed each other with so much more facility as the resemblance between them is the more striking, and more difficult in the contrary position.

We should never come to a conclusion were we to enter into a discussion on the approximation and removal of all the passions : let us select *one,* however, for our contemplation ; that of choler, for instance, in those points in which it belongs to other affections, and to that let us apply our theory to establish its justice. If it be demanded why the contemplation in his own proper merit, in his courage, or in his strength, renders the man more inclined to choler than any other contemplative, tranquil affection ? the answer immediately presents itself, whilst we consider the situation in which this proud sentiment places the soul. Plenitude, energy, and firmness are already situated in the mind; nought is wanting but a celerity in the increase, carried almost to fury, and the soul will be mounted to the pitch when it is ready to burst suddenly into choler.

Do we wish to know why joy, however apparently the opposite of choler, is likewise transmuted with the greatest facility when it is carried to excess? (An observation whose truth is confirmed by the frequent quarrels attendant on the noisy orgies of Bacchus;) the nature of the march of the ideas will furnish an equal solution of this problem: joy, too highly exalted, acquires so great, so unquiet a celerity, its march is so firm, it darts forward with so much vigour, that one greater degree of tension suffices to transmute it into the sentiment of choler. I own that my explanation may be far from satisfactory, and I hope, my friend, that this confession will not surprise you: in truth I have here only attached myself to the most general possibilities of a respective connexion between the different affections: but you, doubtless, well remember that, from the commencement of these researches, I have limited and confined them.

Once more consider the subjects with a little attention, and they will furnish matter for some important remarks. The first will be, that the approach or removal, which may exist between

the affections, does not depend so much upon
their nature in general as on their respective
force.   To prove that grief and melancholy are
remote affections, between whom no mediate
tint can intervene, it would not suffice me to
name them entirely unique, but it is necessary
that, considering them in their superior degrees,
I should select grief, accompanied with fury, and
the most profound melancholy.   Whilst these
affections subsist in an inferior degree, there is
scarcely any difficulty in passing from the one
to the other.   He who, beaten down by grief,
sadly leans on the tomb of the friend he has just
lost, feels at once the force of the grief with
which he is overpowered.   In the act of heaving
a profound sigh, he raises his eyes, swimming
with tears, to heaven, and after having procured
this slight relief for his bursting heart, he falls
again into his pristine melancholy.   His muscles
suddenly lose their momentary tension, and the
head falls on the bosom.

It was necessary that I should determine all
the other affections more particularly, in the
same manner, to render their removal sensible.
It was necessary that I should depict love soft
and tender, joy lively and animated, admiration
full and mixed with astonishment, choler impe-

tuous, and approaching towards fury. In my opinion, we should do well were we to speak of the proximity of several emotions, several passionate conditions of the soul, instead of many and *diverse* affections. This last mode of expression engages us too easily to occupy ourselves solely with the idea of a particular species, and hinders us from carrying our attention to the entire and specific situation in which the soul then finds itself placed. To this remark another immediately suggests itself: *i. e.* that in the examination of the proximity of the movements of the soul, we should not be too much attached to the ordinary mode of expressing ourselves, though it be frequently that which is employed by the language of philosophy.

This method does not always designate the passions with an adequate exactitude; sometimes, instead of indicating a mixture, it solely makes mention of the predominant affection. Thus it is said, the jealous man suddenly relapses from the most desperate fury into the most soft and melting love. Examine the character of *Othello*, which offers such a complete and perfect picture of jealousy. What do you find in the scene where the Moor, after having talked with so much violence to his wife, is suddenly attract-

ed by the irresistible impulse of her charms?
no other thing but emotions, which are carried
almost to tenderness; then a sudden explosion
of the most rending grief, of which love is the
probable source, but which offer neither trace
nor suspicion of the characteristical movements
of this passion. You may likewise remember
that, in a scene with Iago, after having declared
his firm resolution of taking away the life of
Desdemona, he recalls all her beauties—her soft,
engaging manners; in a word, all her natural
perfections, to his mind. What do you here
perceive more than an interior emotion, replete
with secret anguish; than a sufferance as lively
as profound, from which he is liable to replunge,
every moment into that original furor which
urges him on to vengeance?—a transition which
could not take place if his heart was moved by a
veritable tenderness. Love is doubtless the fundamental affection which causes these violent
emotions in the soul, but even these emotions
have nothing of that softness, that tender languor, which characterise this sentiment. My
third remark will go to prove that the facility of
connexion between all the approaching passions
is not reciprocal. The transition of choler to
grief, and from grief to choler, is equally easy

and rapid; but the return from choler to joy,
or to the proud and tranquil sentiment of self-
grandeur, is a step more difficult and uneasy
than that of these last affections to the former.
It is here with the movements of the soul as with
the waves of the sea; the tempest must doubtless have been displayed some time ere it could
have penetrated the depths of the ocean or
elevated the billows to the skies; but it must
require much more before the agitated waters
can subside to a calm, or present the aspect of a
smooth and gently gliding undulation. This
comparison, as you will easily remark, cannot
be applied either to choler or grief; the one of
these affections is as impetuous as the other,
and, by a natural consequence, the transitions
are equally easy.

The precedent discussion proves to you, that
what has been said of the movements of the soul
of one kind can also be applied to those of a
different species, whether they are *connected or
removed*. The succession of the former, if the
march of their ideas is not entirely the same,
consists solely in an insensible increase or dimi-
nution, whether in the celerity, in the plenitude,
in the stability, or in the equality of this march,
or in several of these qualities at once.   The im-

mediate succession of those movements of the
soul, which are at a distance from each other,
would be to overleap a boundary; and this
Nature never attempts, either in the intellectual
sphere or the corporeal world.   Every thing is
connected in its operation by chains (often, in
truth, almost imperceptible); and when we think
she has broken through vast intervals, it is only
because the invisible link has eluded our penetration : similar violent transitions then are impossible.   The rapid torrent of the thoughts can
neither be suddenly arrested, nor can their slow
and silent pace be accelerated on the instant :
still less can we momentarily vary the different
qualities which we have remarked in their succession.   A certain disorder, an unquiet fluctuation between the condition which is about to
terminate and that which is ready to begin, will
here take place, as well as in the connexions of
the movements of the soul, of which the species
are the same, though the degrees are farther removed.   While the distance which exists between
the affections is very small, it is nearly the same
as if these affections were closely allied.   When
the separation is considerable, then the agitation, the oscillation, and the efforts of the soul,
affected of two incompatible sentiments, will

become perceptible to the organs of sight by
the modifications which the body will undergo.
Here we may remark, according to the variety
of the cases, sometimes the bursts of laughter,
sometimes the convulsions of tears, sometimes
the alteration of the colour of the face, a sudden
trembling of all the members, that unquiet agitation which discovers doubt, uneasiness, or other
indecisive and uncertain movements of this kind.
In the art of declamation, the different changes
and breaks in the tone answer to these modifications of pantomime. You perhaps suspect that
I am about to trace with you the *prodigious
field* which now extends itself to our curiosity—
if not through the whole, at least a great part of
it; but, to my great regret, all that I can here
say reduces itself to remarks partly trivial and
partly indeterminate; and I candidly avow my
want of skill to develope with exactitude and
precision the more fine and less generally known
observations which the subject presents on every
side. I have only indicated, in a general way,
those differences which exist in the march of the
ideas proper to each affection, as well as those
which characterise the modifications of laughter,
tears, trembling; and with how much precision
would it be requisite to determine each of these

differences? with what exactness it would be needful to indicate in the former the proportion of their infinitely varied qualities; and in the other, their degrees and deviations. Nevertheless, it was not idle in me to present this kind of speculation to a mind like yours, solicitous for the acquisition of knowledge. Though this may be but a faint outline, it may still, even under its present form, prove of some utility to the artist, in exciting him to seek for the gesture, mien, and attitude proper to each situation, in giving him a taste for a kind of observation, whose reunion and comparison, spite of all the obstacles which here present themselves, may, in the end, procure him a knowledge more exact and more solid than we have hitherto attained in the various contemplations of so difficult a subject.

LETTER XXXVI.

Comparison of Mr. Hume—The Subject discussed—Difficulty of distinguishing the more fine Vibrations of the Passions —Examples—Alcestis, Phædra, &c.

You will find a dissertation in Hume upon the subject of the passions, which to me appears extremely beautiful, and more rich than Home on the same subject. The first of these authors compares the soul to an instrument with strings, which, being struck upon, continue their vibrations after the impulse has ceased, and decrease by little and little in an almost imperceptible degree.

"If we consider the human mind, we shall observe that, with regard to the passions, it is not like a wind instrument of music, which, in running over all the notes, immediately loses the sound when the breath ceases; but rather resembles a string instrument, where, after each stroke, the vibrations still retain some sound, which gradually and insensibly decays. The imagination is extremely quick and agile; but the passions, in comparison, are slow and restive: for which reason, when any object is presented which affords a variety of views to the one and emotions to the other, though the fancy may change its views with great celerity, each stroke will not produce a clear and distinct note of passion, but the one passion will always be mixed and confounded with the other."—*Essays and Treatises on several Subjects.*

For this reason, the tones immediately following the original ones are never quite pure; the new vibrations are extended with the first, which yet last; and the tones are thus mingled and confounded one with the other. After the same rule, the affections, which ought rapidly to succeed to each other, can seldom be pure ones. The situation in which the soul has been placed by the former affection yet lasts, while the new one is just commencing, and till its effect ceases. Home, who simply speaks of the tone of the soul, without a more precise determination, leaves us in uncertainty, if his comparison is taken from the sound of the flute, which vanishes with the cessation of the breath.

You exhort me not to be sparing of my examples whenever they are absolutely necessary; and with this exhortation I find myself induced to comply.

I shall confine myself, however, in this article, and give you but a few of them, merely to demonstrate that the subject of our mutual researches may be made of some practical utility, and to encourage reflecting artists to multiply their observations on this interesting matter: these examples need not contain any great subtilty. I have complained several times already, that, in designating the too feeble shades of the passions, language is unable to afford clear, appropriate expressions for them.

The first example which at present presents itself to me is taken from a story pretty generally known: I allude to the dramatic piece called *Alcestis*.

ALCESTIS, who, to save her husband, has devoted herself, by a solemn vow, to the infernal gods, is suddenly struck with the terrible idea that she already hears the beating wings of the subterraneous shades, and that she sees them approaching, to drag her away as their consecrated victim. The composer, who developes these ideas by the repetition of the same motive, makes the horror of this queen increase from

word to word : pauses, judiciously managed, successively render her respiration more short ; and
the *piano*, gradually augmented, insensibly sti-
fles her voice.—The last attitude of an actress
charged with such a part should accompany this
expression with a degree of faintness almost approaching to annihilation, with her face averted
from the spot whence the terrific sounds are supposed to arise : she should now and then cast
a timid and furtive glance, as if fearful of beholding the dreaded spectres : the reversed hands,
which she had opposed to them, ought to preserve their former direction ; but she should not
appear to have force or courage sufficient to give
any degree of tension to the muscles, so that,
feeble and trembling, they may afterwards drop
lifeless by her sides.   *(See Plate* XLVII.)

Immediately after this weakness caused by fear,
the second invocation of the infernal gods and·
the devotion of this faithful wife ought to take
place.   The musical declamation is here replete
with animation and a kind of savage enthusiasm : she should indicate a soul displaying its
greatest degrees of energy ; and the play ought
consequently to acquire a superior degree of
vivacity.   The countenance of Alcestis should
be fixed on the ground, because she is invoking

the infernal deities; her body should bend forwards; her step ought to be grand, her arms
extend, and each open eye to seem bursting
from its orbit: the whole countenance should
beam with a species of haggard inspiration.
(See Plate XLVIII.)   Each of these expressions, separately taken, are exactly conformable
to truth; as much in respect to the words which
they ought to accompany, as to the situation of
the soul, which they are intended to designate:
neither of these can be called too strong nor too
weak.   But to be more rapid in the transitions,
to rush on from weakness to strength, or from
strength to weakness, with a kind of instantaneous celerity, would be to act directly contrary to
the knowledge which even the most uninstructed
spectator has attained of the human heart, and
of the nature of sentiments in general. It is here
necessary to introduce a pause, and even a very
long one, to connect and bind together sentiments so extremely opposite to their intermediate conditions.

Parthenia, in supporting the Queen, who is
ready to fall, should clasp her sister closely in her
arms.   Alcestis, reposing on her faithful bosom,
should soon recover herself, and lifting up her
feeble arm, in the sentiment of the disorder

which troubles her soul, should draw her hand
across her forehead ; whilst Parthenia, with looks
replete with love and grief, should appear to con-
jure her to abandon her design, and revoke the
dreadful vow she has just been pronouncing.
(See Plate XLIX.)   As her spirits and strength
return, all the tenderness of Alcestis should likewise revive.   Unshaken in her resolution, she
ought, at first, solely to avert her looks from
Parthenia ; immediately after, her hand, placed
in that of her sister, should begin to tremble ;
her attempts to tear herself from her arms should
afterwards become more strong, and her eyes, as
well as her forehead, should express a certain
secret displeasure with the most noble persever-
ance : but after the most tender looks and embraces, the Queen, too strongly attached to her
heroic devotion, should tear herself entirely from
the arms of Parthenia.   *(See Plate* L.)   And it
is here that another invocation of the infernal
Gods ought to ensue.   By this means the repetition of this devotion will be found not only
perfect, but the hurried leap from one sentiment
to the other will be totally avoided ; and what,
without this prudent precaution, might have appeared a useless ornament or a mere misplaced,

musical luxury, becomes an admirable and expressive trait in the character of Alcestis.

The art of passing adroitly from one movement to the other is very difficult, particularly when these movements destroy each other with an extreme rapidity. Orosmane, in Voltaire's Zaire, is at one time hurried on by passion ; at another, he is an unfortunate lover, whose betrayed love exhales itself in bitter complaints. This sentiment, and the desire of vengeance, alternately govern his whole soul ; but love, so closely united to choler, can only manifest itself under the semblance of grief; and as we have remarked, the reciprocal transition of one of these two sentiments to the other is extremely easy.

LETTER XXXVII.

The Conclusion.

HITHERTO, my friend, we have been reasoning upon simple sentiments, or at least upon such as are apparently so. There still remains one circumstance for us to examine, to wit, that where several sentiments already exist in the soul, of which one may assume the ascendancy, without the least disorder resulting from all the others. It is evident that we may here apply the same principles, of which we have availed ourselves in appreciating the changes of the simple sentiments : thus you must not expect many new or important observations upon this subject.

If the affection which ought to acquire the preponderancy already governs the composed passion, it will only stand in need of a little re-inforcement to make the concomitant affection entirely disappear. I readily agree, that (as you

have remarked) my reflexions only extend to
generals, without stopping to characterise par-
ticulars.   I have also read the work you were so
good as to point out to me, and have found it
worthy of its judicious author.   It contains the
solution of a question which had long perplexed
me.

"The quick passage from one contrary to
another," says M. Tiedermann, "explains itself
very easily.   When the operations give rise to a
sudden change in the determinate causes, *laughter* and *choler* (not the bitter laugh of disdain,
but that of joy and gladness), reciprocally ex-
clude each other, notwithstanding the man, animated with the most violent choler, cannot
restrain himself from the most hearty laughter,
at the moment when his adversary, no longer
opposing him with resistance, manifests his fear,
or his inferiority, by comic attitude, and this
even when an equal motive would not have
created laughter in another situation.   The idea
of the contrast, between the impetuous developement of his own powers and the feeble resistance he experiences, leads him irresistibly on to
laughter; and it is not insensibly, but in a sud-

den way, that he thus passes from one contrary
to another."

If the question here was not that of a man
animated with the most violent choler, I should
contest neither the justice nor the truth of this
observation.   But I am at a loss to conceive
how a sudden, vehement, and decided choler
can pass with such rapidity to violent bursts of
laughter.   In whatever point of view I contemplate this situation, it appears to me, precisely,
that because a man of honour forgets his anger
against a *coward*, he finds he ought to be vexed
with himself, and manifest his internal discon-
tent by his words or his actions; so that, if he
permits himself to laugh, it will necessarily be
with bitterness—the laugh of *disdain* and *contempt*, not that of gaiety and joy.   But, granting
the observation of this author to be true, it does
not seem to prove the fact which we are now
discussing; to wit, the possibility of a sudden
passage from one contrary to the other.   The
true contrary of choler ought to be a sentiment
which, instead of a process hurried, impetuous,
and full of irregularity, should assume one more
slow, feeble, and uniform; and the most perfect
contrary would be that which united all these

properties in a supreme degree: but this is not the case of laughter, which indicates an intermediate sentiment, a species of indecision and certain fluctuation of the soul, more approximating to gay and lively sentiments than to the indolent and impetuous affections. The angry man who should pass suddenly from fury to fits of laughter would not, for all this, bound from one extreme to the other: he would solely fall into a *fluctuation*, which would tend to incline him towards the contrary sentiment, though, I own, with a certain rapidity.

" In the same manner," continues M. Tiedermann, " a violent love changes into hatred, when we find the object unworthy of future affection, and when a long enjoyment has not prepared the way to indifference. The force of our attachment makes us perceive, in so much a more lively manner, the baseness and unworthiness of the subject; and impels us on to the most vehement hatred, in making us pass the bounds of *indifference*."

Shylock, in the Merchant of Venice, affords a fine example to illustrate transitions of passions and affections.

Shylock experiences the most bitter anguish, whilst recalling to his mind the precious jewels he has lost by the flight of his daughter: he evinces the most lively joy, whilst learning the catastrophe of Antonio, his rival in commerce, on whom he feels he can revenge himself at his pleasure.   Accordingly, as his friend Tubal directs the attention of Shylock to the one or the other of these events, these two opposite sentiments alternately succeed in the soul of the Jew: grief seems to take the place of joy, and joy to assume that of grief, without any intermediate sentiment.   I use the word *seems*, since grief, in succeeding to joy, no longer manifests itself with the same violence as in its original; and so joy, likewise, in its sudden triumph over grief, cannot, in its first instants, efface the wrinkles from the forehead, and restore it to all its natural serenity.   With a feeble light, it smiles, as we may say, through a cloud, still leaving something of pain and chagrin in the first mien, and probably in the first tone of Shylock's voice; but the essential circumstance to be observed here is, that in joy there is found an accessary sentiment, which serves for its point of union with grief: I mean that joy arising from the misery of another person; consequently the joy of *hatred* (of choler moderated) so closely approaches grief. The two alternate sentiments are not then simple, though they appear to be so.——But we are beginning to lose ourselves in subtilties, which appear to remove farther and farther from us in practice. It is time then to terminate our researches, and to end our correspondence.

If you find that I have furnished but little, recollect that I never promised much; yet I dare flatter myself with having done more than my promise obliged me to execute. Instead of merely collecting a few materials for the edifice, and leaving them as rude as I found them, I have, at least, in connecting them in some sort among themselves, elevated a vast though imperfect monument, open on all sides, and perhaps menacing ruin. It is very probable that a construction so precipitate, and so incomplete, should moulder of itself, or that some destructive critique should level it with the dust: but a hope constantly remains, to cheer and console me——a hope that, in the end, an architect of superior talent will find the *site* which I have chosen not only very agreeable, but also very advantageously disposed for the increase of our acquirements as well as our pleasures; and that, on the same spot where I have constructed a frail edifice to an art which I love, a majestic temple may arise, whose well ordered parts shall be decorated with all the graces of taste and all the sublimities of regular magnificence.

APPENDIX.

———

Some account of the dresses now worn on the London theatres will be a useful addition to this work. It may prove a source of pleasurable curiosity to foreign artists; and may afford some slight degree of amusement to such persons as reside in provincial towns, and whose avocations do not allow them to make periodical visits to the metropolis.

Every one knows that Thespis was the founder of that art which has since evinced itself the parent of heroic virtue and the ornament of polished nations; but nothing could be more miserable than the *habits* and decorations of these original actors. The celebrated Roman satirist thus forcibly describes the apparatus, wardrobe, and machinery:

Ignotum tragicæ genus invenisse Camœnæ
Dicitur, et *plaustris* vexisse poemata Thespis,
Quæ canerent agerentque, peruncti fæcibus ora.

Horace.

Translated thus by Francis :

> Thespis, inventor of the tragic art,
> Carried his vagrant players in a cart;
> High o'er the crowd the mimic tribe appear'd,
> And play'd and sung, with lees of wine besmear'd.

In tracing the improvements of dress and theatrical costume, the name of Æschylus follows
in regular progression after that of Thespis.
Æschylus may indeed be termed the real father
of the stage.   Horace has mentioned the orna-
mental advantages which he added to the rough
sketches of his predecessor :

> Post hunc personæ, pallæque repertor honestæ
> Æschylus, et modicis instravit pulpita tignis,
> Et docuit magnumque loqui, nitique cothurno.

> Then Æschylus a decent *vizard* used,
> Built a low stage, the flowing *robe* diffused :
> In language more sublime his actors rage,
> And in the graceful *buskin* tread the stage.

When we consider how greatly he improved
the scenic and mechanical parts of the theatre,
we may very fairly give him credit for all the
steps which have since been taken for the perfection of departments so essential and material.
This great man had too much knowledge of the
human heart, not to feel assured that sensible

objects strike most forcibly on the imagination ; and that the active principle of the human mind could not easily be abstracted from its own concerns by a cold, dry narrative of unembellished facts. His good sense told him that a tragedy personified in mean habiliments would every moment forcibly recall to the minds of the multitude that it was not a king, a general, or an ambassador, but a mere player, who was making his appeal to their passions. The " docuit magnum loqui " was one of his great merits; the " nitique cothurno " ought not to be reckoned among his least. When his play of the Eumenides was first acted, it is reported that many children were frightened to death ; and the female part of the audience so forcibly affected that they were carried away in violent convulsions. This incident *alone* is a striking proof of the vast improvement he must have made in the articles of costume and dress.

We have said that he added the robe and the mask to the decorations of the drama. The use of the *robe* may be easily conceived : it gave a dignity to the whole figure ; and afforded the actors many opportunities for the display of a superior taste, by the graceful folds into which they could convert it at their pleasure. Many of

the ancient statues and pictures owe their highest
charm to the disposition of the drapery.

The masks are of so ancient an origin that we
find a difficulty in tracing them to their primitive invention.   It is pretty evident, however,
that Æschylus was the first who ever adapted
them to the purposes of the drama.   Masks, as
used upon the ancient stages, covered the whole
head; they represented the hair, the eyebrows,
the lips, &c. &c.   The different passions of the
human soul were likewise depicted on them; and
masks of love, joy, hope, frenzy, despair, and
pride were formed by an able artist for the different characters, as they happened to be requisite in various plays.   Furies, satyrs, fauns, har-
pies, &c. were likewise represented by a skilful
constructor of these articles, to the highest delight and gratification of an audience.   Many
conveniences were the result of this practice,
conveniences which greatly counterbalanced the
arguments that have been so repeatedly urged
against it.   A performer did not then suffer so
materially from those ravages which the hand of
time will inevitably make upon the finest set of
features.   As long as the organs of utterance
were unimpaired, the wrinkles of age were but
slight impediments to the efforts of an accom-

plished actor, even in the trying task of sustain-
ing and supporting characters of vigorous juve-
nility. Several of their plays were formed on
plots similar to that of our immortal countryman
in his Comedy of Errors. Amphytrion and the
Menechmæ afford instances of this nature. We
have never seen two men so exactly conformable
in their physical appearances as to be enabled
to represent the Dromios of Shakspeare in a way
that could mislead our senses or bewilder our
imaginations even for a moment; yet we can
conceive it highly probable that two personages,
at the immense distance which divided the actors
of Greece from their auditors, might, by the aid
of masks exactly similar, keep up the illusion of
the senses, and give a double zest to plots of
such a texture. We learn, likewise, by every
description of the masks, that the Grecian theatres were of a prodigious size, even when compared with the large ones which have been lately
erected in our own and neighbouring countries.
For this reason the masks were considerably larger
than the human head, so that when diminished
by distance they might bear a proportionable
appearance.

We are also informed that the actors had instruments within the hollow portions of their

masks so contrived that the vibration of sound might convey what they had to recite, to persons placed at the extremities of their theatres. Without the assistance of these masks and instruments to the vocal energies, the audiences of Greece and Rome must have been the mere spectators of tedious, faint, and inanimate pantomimes.

The words *sock* and *buskin* are so familiar to every ear that it is perhaps unnecessary to mention, that the one designated a tragic, and the other a comic performance.

Shakspeare was to England what Æschylus was to ancient Greece; every thing before his time, relative to the drama, is buried in confusion and obscurity. In Shakspeare's time there were seven principal theatres, but all his plays were most probably acted at the theatres of the Globe and Blackfriars. That the article of *dress* had then made some improvement is very evident from the following passage :

" The person who spoke the prologue, who entered immediately after the third sounding, usually wore a long, black velvet cloak; which, I suppose, was considered as best adapted to a supplicatory address. Of this custom, whatever may have been its origin, some traces remained till very lately; a black coat having been, if I mistake not, within these few years, the constant stage-habiliment of our modern prologue speakers. The complete dress of the ancient prologue-speaker is still retained in the play exhibited in Hamlet, before the king and court of Denmark." Again: " The stage-dresses, it is reasonable to suppose, were much more costly in some play-houses than others; yet the wardrobe of even the king's servants, at the *Globe* and *Blackfriars*, was, we find, but scantily furnished, and our author's dramas derived but very *little* aid from the *splendour* of exhibition."

" In Sir William D'Avenant's company, from the time their new threatre was opened, in Portugal Row, near Lincoln's Inn Fields (April, 1662), the total receipt (after deducting the nightly charges of men, hirelings, and other customary charges) was divided into fifteen shares; of which it was agreed, by articles previously entered into, that ten should belong to D'Avenant, viz. two towards the house-rent, building, scaffolding, and making of frames for scenes; one for a provision of *habits*, *properties*, and scenes, for a supplement to the said theatre, &c."—

Vide Historical Account of the English Stage, in Johnson's and Steevens's Shakspeare, Prolegomena, Vol. II.

Much curious information may be obtained on this head from a perusal of the life of Colley Cibber. The dress of Cato is particularized by a very eminent poet; who describes the gown and *wig* worn by Booth, the original representative of that character, in a very accurate manner. It may afford some scope for speculation on the progression of dress, to remark, that the very suit of clothes worn by Wilks as the airy, lively, dashing Sir Harry Wildair, is at the *present moment* the habit adopted by the antiquated, formal, star-gazing Old Foresight, in the admirable comedy of Love for Love.

To Mr. Garrick the stage owes great obligation; and his memory will be dear to the lovers of the drama as long as the works of Shakspeare continue to be the admiration of a British audience: yet in tracing the progression of dress, we may surely be permitted to make a few passing observations, without detracting from the merit of that *immortal man*. There was nothing ridiculous in *his* wearing a *wig* in the character of Ranger, but such a dress would now excite the risible faculties of the audience. The characters of Macbeth and Romeo, which he represented so perfectly, would have been improved by the Scottish and the Italian garb. King Richard is said to have been so exquisitely delineated by this great actor that none but those who had the happiness of seeing him can form any idea of the sublimity of his conception of that arduous part. The dress of Richard was as correct then as it is at present; but the other characters were attired in embroidered coats and waistcoats, cocked hats, powered heads, bags, and court swords. The general effect must have been considerably impaired by such a distinction; and with an actor of less ability, the illusion would have been weakened, if not destroyed: but while Garrick acted, attention was employed on him, and him alone; all exterior objects were put to flight by his transcendant genius.

It will be generally allowed, that the actors of the present day maintain a decided superiority over their predecessors in the art of dressing their characters, and in a strict attention to costume. Trifling as this advantage may appear when opposed to the more noble portions of the drama, its importance will be readily admitted by the real connoisseur. When Macbeth appears

on the wild heath, with his plaid-covered chief-
tains, is not the fiction more aided by the sub-
stitution of the warlike Caledonian garb than
when he marched down the stage with a powder-
ed head and a gold-laced coat and waistcoat?
When Alexander the Great was attired in silk
stockings, was it not a total violation of history,
truth, and propriety ?

These examples will speak for themselves; and
to those who are dubious of the assertion which
gives the palm to modern performers, in the articles of dress and costume, the sketches placed at
the end of this work will be the best reply.

REPROACH.

Plate LI. represents Queen Kathraine in the trial scene, in the play of Henry VIII. She is in the attitude of reproaching the king and the cardinal for the accumulated injuries which have been heaped upon her head :

Wolsey. Be patient yet.
 Q. Kath. I will when you are humble—nay, before,
Or God will punish me. I do believe,
Induced by potent circumstances, that
You are mine enemy; and make my challenge ;
You shall not be my judge, for it is you
Have blown this coal betwixt my lord and me—
Which God's dew quench! therefore I say again,
I utterly abhor, yea, from my soul
Refuse you for my judge ; whom yet once more
I hold my most malicious foe, and think him
Not at all a friend to truth.

Often to place with vehemence the right fist on the left palm is an action commonly employed by those who mock, chide, insult, reproach, rebuke, and explode, or drive out with noise. Vulgar persons use it in their bickerings, as being the scold's taunting dialect and the natural

rhetoric of those who declaim at Billingsgate.
Ovid, not unskilful in this brawling property of
the hand, ingeniously metamorphoses the Pieri-
des, as they were about to scold and clap their
hands, into pies and silvan scolds.

SUPPLICATION.

Plate LII. represents Queen Katharine in an attitude of supplication. It is taken from a scene in the first act of the tragedy of King Henry VIII.

A noise within, crying, " Room for the Queen." *Enter the Queen, ushered by the Dukes of Norfolk and Suffolk. She kneels. The King riseth from his state, takes her up, kisses and placeth her by him.*

Q. *Kath.* Nay, we must longer kneel—
I am a suitor.

The stretching forth and clasping the hands, when we importunately entreat, sue, beseech, or ask mercy, is the gesture of supplication. Thus the Romans, who sued in behalf of Coriolanus, used this gesture, when Sicenius the tribune had pronounced sentence of death upon him, holding forth their hands to the people, beseeching them not to sacrifice this noble Roman. Thus Manlius and Fulvius came to Tiberius with tears in their eyes, and holding up their hands, besought him to leave the Agrarian law unaltered.

Plutarch, in the description of the triumph of Emilius, relates that King Perses' children were led in with their masters, officers, and other servants, weeping and lamenting, holding out their hands, that they might appear to ask mercy and grace from the people as they passed in the triumphal procession. The power of this expression has sometimes remained in the arm, even when the hand has been lost. When the people of Athens were about to stone Æschylus the tragedian for some impiety which he had brought upon the stage, his brother Amynias, who had lost his hand at the battle of Salamis, held up his arm, which reminding the judges of the services of Amynias, they immediately acquitted the poet. This gesture may be often observed in children, when entreating forgiveness; and Raffaelle has adopted it with great success in the figure of our Saviour in the Transfiguration.

In prayer which ranks next to supplication, to raise the hands joined and hollowed in the middle, or spread towards heaven, is the habit of devotion, and a natural and universal form of prayer. This is the language of contrition, submission, entreaty, and supplication. Alexander, in his third battle with Darius, before charging the enemy, grasped his lance in his left hand, and extending his right, besought the gods to assist him, and to encourage the Grecians. The

Heathens also, when they came forth to plough, laid one hand upon the stilt of the plough, and lifted the other up to Ceres; beginning their actions both of war and peace with the same gesture. " Sustulit excitas vinelis ad sydera palmas."

The ancients are very copious in expressing these outward forms of devotion in the hands. They say, the hands stretched out, expanded, and erected, all naturally imply this expression. With Tertullian, the hands thus affected are expanded; with Virgil holden abroad; as Nonnius interpreteth the action, they are the open and extended hands. Cresollius says, this deportment of our hands declares that we affectionately fly unto the protection of our heavenly father, as little children when alarmed, with stretched out hands, run into the lap of their parents, or as men in the midst of a shipwreck stretch out their hands to some friendly Saviour. In a medal of Gordian, there is a figure raising its expanded hands with this inscription " Pietas Augusta," and, according to Eusebius, Constantine was represented in coins and paintings with his hands extended forth. The Romish church superabounds in the external expressions of devotion, some of which have been quaintly commented upon by

the old writers; for instance, Huelamus, in his
gloss upon the " Oremus" in the Romish mass,
says, that by the extension of his hands the priest
gathers, as it were, the hearts of the people; and,
by conjoining of them, unites them into one. It
is the custom of mothers to teach their children
this gesture at their devotion; and of this idea
Sir Joshua Reynolds availed himself in his beautiful little picture of the infant Samuel.

FALLEN GREATNESS.

For an illustration of this attitude represented in *Plate* LIII. the reader will refer to Scene II. Act 3. of Henry VIII.

K. Hen. ....Read o'er this :   [*Giving him papers.*
And, after, this : and then to breakfast, with
What appetite you may.
    [*Exit King, frowning upon Cardinal Wolsey: the Nobles
        throng after him, smiling and whispering.*
  Wolsey. What should this mean?
What sudden anger's this?   How have I reap'd it?
He parted frowning from me, as if ruin
Leap'd from his eyes : so looks the chafed lion
Upon the daring huntsman that has gall'd him.
Then makes him nothing.   I must read this paper;
I fear the story of his anger.—'Tis so ;
This paper hath undone me :—'tis the account
Of all that world of wealth I have drawn together
For mine own ends : indeed to gain the popedom,
And for my friends in Rome.   O negligence
Fit for a fool to fall by!   What cross devil
Made me put this main secret in the packet
I sent the king?   Is there no way to cure this?
No new device, to beat this from his brains?
I know, 'twill stir him strongly, yet I know
A way, if it take right, in spite of fortune,
Will bring me off again.   What's this—*To the Pope?*
The letter, as I live, with all the business
I writ to his holiness.—Nay, then, farewell!
I have touch'd the highest point of all my greatness, &c.

SICKNESS.

Queen Katharine, Henry VIII. *(See Plate* LIV.)

Enter Katharine dowager, sick; led between Griffith and Patience.

　Griffith. How does your grace ?
　Kath. O Griffith, sick to death :
My legs, like loaded branches, bow to the earth,
Willing to leave their burden : Reach a chair.—
Patience, be near me still, and set me lower :
I have not long to trouble thee.—Good Griffith,
Cause the musicians play me that sad note
I named my knell, whilst I sit meditating
On that celestial harmony.

CONCEIT.

Plate LV. is intended to designate the character of Sir Abel Handy in the comedy of Speed the Plough. Sir Abel Handy is an old gentleman, who is so conceited of his own skill, in every thing that relates to mechanical inventions, that he invariably mars his own ideas, in the execution of his favourite plans. He carries his lady's fan in his cane, &c. &c. To delineate the character, as depicted by its late representative, exceeds the power of graphic illustration ; it is one of the most humorous efforts of as excellent a comic actor as ever graced the boards of a theatre : one whose talents have been so long acknowledged, by sound critics, that any farther encomium, in this place, would be as presumptuous as it is unnecessary.

Sir Abel. Better and better—" the whole capable of the greatest improvement." Come, that seems true, however.— I shall have plenty to do, that's one comfort—I'll have such contrivances ! I'll have a canal run through my kitchen—I

must give this rustic some idea of my consequence. [*Aside.*]
You must know, farmer, you have the honour of conversing
with a man who has obtained patents for tweezers, tooth-
picks, and tinder-boxes—to a philosopher who has been con-
sulted on the Wapping docks and the Gravesend tunnel, and
who has now in hand two inventions which will render him
immortal—the one is for converting sawdust into deal boards,
and the other is a plan for cleaning rooms by a steam engine
—and, farmer, I mean to give prizes for industry—I'll have a
ploughing match.

VULGAR TRIUMPH.

Plate LVI. represents Dame Ashfield in the comedy of Speed the Plough. In the wife of a simple farmer, we here behold the passion of envy as forcibly portrayed as it could possibly be evinced in the more exalted situations of human life. If a misfortune happens to her family, her greatest affliction is to anticipate the triumph Mrs. Grundy will enjoy. If events are favourable, her satisfaction is augmented to the highest pitch, in the idea of the mortification it will occasion Mrs. Grundy. She is here in an attitude of extreme exultation. The son of a baronet has just offered his hand in marriage to her daughter. Far from reflecting on the advantages such an unlooked-for event would bring to her only child, her mind dwells with rapture on the idea of plaguing her rustic competitor; and, in the full torent of impetuous joy, she proudly makes use of her constant exclamation—What will Mrs. Grundy say?

HOPELESS LOVE.

Plate LVII. represents the character of Octavian, very generally known: the play of the Mountaineers being frequently performed at the three theatres of the metropolis. Every one who has read Don Quixote must acknowledge the similarity between Octavian in the play and Cardenio in the romance. It is most probable that the costume of Cardenio, as described by Cervantes, though delightful in the novel, would have proved disgusting in a theatre. His smeared face, matted locks, and wounded limbs would have offered too terrific a picture for dramatic exhibition, as now personified. The dress here copied is sufficiently striking, without offering any thing which might disgust the eyes or shock the hearts of the spectators. Octavian is bending, in hopeless love, over the mimic features of his beloved mistress.

Sweet Floranthe!
When the cold limner drew thy semblance here,
How pleased I sat, to mark the modest flush
Which virgin nature threw upon thy cheek,
As the dull clod unmoved did stare upon thee,
To pencil out thy features' character!
Those times are past, Floranthe.

Mountaineers, Act 3.

VULGAR ASTONISHMENT.

THE character represented in *Plate* LVIII. is Dan, in the comedy of John Bull. Dan is looking with surprise at Peregrine, the traveller, who has just declared that he had drunk " Burgundy with the French, Hollands with the Dutch," &c. &c.

Dan. Dang me, but he is a rum customer! it's my opinion he'll take a fancy to our sour beer.

OBSEQUIOUSNESS.

Doctor Panglos (in the Comedy of the Heir at Law) is represented in *Plate* LIX. in the act of offering his services, for three hundred pounds a year, to *any body* that will accept of them; and is supposed to be concluding a most humorous final speech with the following couplets :—

> If any body wants a tutor here,
> My terms are just three hundred pounds a year;
> Upon my merits I shall lay no stress,
> I am an LL. D. and an ASS.
> On their own virtues modest men are dumb--
> Plaudite et valete—Terence.— Hum !

RUSTIC CUNNING.

Plate LX, representing Sheepface in the Village Lawyer, is not easily described. The character is that of a country fellow, who, under the appearance of rustic simplicity, carries so much natural cunning that he is an overmatch for the lawyer who has saved him from being transported for sheep-stealing. He is here drawn as standing before the justice on his examination.

Sheepface. Oh! no, don't hang me! Consider, that would be the death of me! besides, your worship, I was only married yesterday; leave me alone for a week or two, and who knows but by that time I may save your worship the trouble.

BAJAZET.

THIS dress was so much admired that it was thought proper to exhibit it in *Plate* LXI. as a specimen of splendid Oriental costume. It represents Bajazet, in the grand ballet of Tamerlane and Bajazet, performed at the Opera House, in the year 1806.

> *Bajazet.* It is beneath me to decline my fate,
> I stand prepared to meet thy utmost hate;
> Yet think not I will long thy triumph see,
> None want the means when the soul dares be free.
> I'll curse thee with my last, my parting breath,
> And keep the courage of my life in death;
> Then boldly venture on a world unknown;
> It cannot use me worse than this has done.

FOPPERY.

Plate LXII. represents Mr. Munden as Jemmy Jumps, in the " Farmer," and is inserted as a specimen of the fashionable habit which then prevailed. The dress and the character are so much dependent on each other that its costume is at present a matter of no small difficulty, and serves to show the contrast in the dress of a beau of 1790 and that of a dandy of 1821.

MIRTH.

The cobler in the Forty Thieves is represented in *Plate* LXIII. singing at his work. The costume is curious, as it displays the great taste of the inventor of the dresses in that splendid spectacle; who has evinced a great portion of taste, by making the dress of the Turkish characters in the subordinate situations of life, as just and appropriate as those of his leaders, captains, and pachas.

AGILITY.

Plate LXIV. represents Morgiana, in the
Forty Thieves, dancing to the Captain of the
Banditti, in the house of Ali Baba.

ADORATION.

Plate LXV. represents Rolla, in the tragedy of Pizarro. He is in the act of adoration, in the Peruvian Temple of the Sun.

Rolla. Yet never was the hour of peril near, when to inspire them words were so little needed. My brave associates —partners of my toil, my feelings, and my fame! Can Rolla's words add vigour to the virtuous energies which inspire your hearts?—No !——

HEARTY WELCOME.

THE figure in *Plate* LXVI. represents Mr. John Moody, in the comedy of the Provoked Husband. He is in the act of shaking hands with Mr. Manly.

Moody. Ads wounds and heart, Measter Manly! I'm glad I ha fun ye. Lawd, Lawd, give me your hand! Why, that's friendly now. Flesh! I thought we would never ha' got hither. Well, and how do you, measter? Good lack! I beg pardon for my bawldness--I did not see as his honour was here.

FASHIONABLE IMPUDENCE.

Tom Shuffleton, in the comedy of John Bull,
is represented in *Plate* LXVII. as addressing
himself to the moral, sententious Peregrine. After
a long lecture from the above gentleman, Shuffleton walks up to him and makes the following
interrogation.

Tom. Pray, Sir, are you a methodist parson, in want of a
congregation ?

Pere. Perhaps, Sir, I am a quack doctor, in want of a
Jack Pudding. Will *you engage* with me ?

A DISCOVERY.

THE sketch in *Plate* LXVIII. is taken from that scene in the comedy of the Dramatist in which Vapid, who had concealed himself under the sofa, overhears the conversation of Lord Scratch and Lady Waitfor't.

Vapid. Prologue or epilogue—I'm the man—I'll write you both.

OBSEQUIOUS ATTENTION.

THE figure in *Plate* LXIX. represents a Spanish
Inn-keeper in the play of the Mountaineers. He
is here in the attitude of soliciting his guest to
order some refreshment ; this guest is a young
lady disguised as a Spanish cavalier. As he leaves
her, he exclaims :

" This is one of your pieces of smock-faced nobility. If
Providence was to rain beards, it would do him no harm to
thrust his chin out into the shower."

INDEX.

INDEX.

INDEX.

ment of pantomime at Carthage, 239. Words should never be resorted to for explaining the gestures of pantomime, 240. Consideration of the assertion that pantomime is now more cramped than it was in the days of Augustus, 242. Pantomimical representation of a part of the story of the Horatii, 245. In order really to interest by pantomime, none but known subjects should be chosen, 246, 247—this, with the necessity of abstaining from the use of words, completely proves the imperfect nature of the art, 250. The senses however may be enriched by it, though the understanding is not, 251. Consideration of the possibility of creating a perfect language of gestures, 251. The perfection ascribed to the ancient pantomimes considered in this view, 258—their real attainment in this respect appreciated, 259. The pantomime language of the modern Sicilians, 260—inference from this example, 261. An objection answered, 262. The spiritless performance of a pantomime produces the same effect as a stupid and prosaic ode, 282.

Paradox, gesture produced by hearing one, 113.

Passions alleged to be susceptible of the same expression in various ways with equal propriety, 4. Importance of a refutation of this opinion, 5. National peculiarities admitted, 5. Particularities of sexual character, and individual qualities, 8. Broad and general basis on which an actor should study the passions, 10, 11. Difficulty of classifying the expressions of the passions, 122, 139. Corporeal sensation expressly distinguished by Descartes from the passions of the soul, 146. The examination of physical effects not to be neglected, 147. Progress of the passions instanced in the example of inattention advancing into a high degree of curiosity, 334—in the approach to choler, 335, 336—in the changes from joy, 336. Comparisons of Hume and of Home on the subject of the passions, 344, 345. See also the article *Affections*.

Peasants express the passions according to their true degree of feeling, 9.

Perjury, dealers in, in the courts of law, 198.

Pherecydes, rythmical structure of his philosophical compositions considered, 278.

Philosophical writing, the rythmical structure of its composition considered, 277, 278.

Physiological gestures described, 44.

Picturesque gestures considered, and their utility exemplified, 31 to 34. Various classes and instances of them, 34 to 40. The union of picturesque with expressive gestures considered; and examples, 215, 220. Picturesque gesture considered as a branch of music, in the ancient Greek acceptation of this word, 264. See further the article *Music*.

Pinching, and gently drawing the garments to and fro, marks of the agonies of death, 15.

Pitchpipe of Gracchus considered, 273.